ENDORSEMENTS

Corey Russell is one of the most genuine men I have ever met. He lives to see Jesus glorified and for people to experience God in the great way we were intended to from the beginning. *Teach Us to Pray* is an amazing tool in helping us understand what it means to seek the Father. We are called to be people that seek Him always! This book walks that out in an amazingly in-depth way.

DEREK CARR
NFL Quarterback for the Las Vegas Raiders

There are few people on the planet that embody the message of intimacy and intercession like Corey Russell. He carries the fiery, prophetic anointing of a modern-day Jeremiah calling the Church back to prayer in the secret place. I am so glad he has written this book, *Teach Us to Pray*, that will serve as a battle plan for a new generation of hungry and thirsty God-seekers.

LEE M. CUMMINGS
Founding & Senior Pastor, Radiant Church
Kalamazoo, Michigan
Author of *Be Radiant* and *FLOURISH: Planting
Your Life Where God Designed It to Thrive*

Now, more than ever, the broader body of Christ is recognizing the crucial importance of prayer. We are realizing how desperately we need to learn how to pray and this book is an answer to those desperate pleas. *Teach Us to Pray* is the heart cry of the church and we're so grateful for faithful intercessors like Corey Russell who are pouring out all they've learned through decades of steadfast prayer.

This book is for those who refuse to go back to normal. It is for those who know there's more than what they've seen in western Christian culture; those unafraid to strip back the many things we thought were so valuable and make space in their days at the feet of Jesus. This is honestly one of the best books on prayer we've ever read. The times are urgent and this book is right on time.

JEREMY and KATIE RIDDLE

Corey Russell's life pursuit and life message is summed up in the title of his latest book *Teach Us to Pray*. For over 20 years, few have pursued a lifestyle of prayer like Corey. His messages on prayer are awakening a generation to the power and simplicity of devoting our lives to the feet of Jesus. This one pursuit is the key to any and every other pursuit. I am forever grateful for the eternal impact of Corey upon my life and the community that I lead.

MICHAEL MILLER
Founder and Lead Pastor of Upper Room Dallas

TEACH US TO PRAY

PRAYER THAT
ACCESSES HEAVEN
AND CHANGES EARTH

COREY RUSSELL

DESTINY IMAGE® PUBLISHERS, INC.

P.O. Box 310, Shippensburg, PA 17257-0310

"Promoting Inspired Lives."

This book and all other Destiny Image and Destiny Image Fiction books are available at Christian bookstores and distributors worldwide.

Cover design by Eileen Rockwell

Interior design by Terry Clifton

For more information on foreign distributors, call 717-532-3040.

Reach us on the Internet: www.destinyimage.com.

ISBN 13 TP: 978-0-7684-5559-5
ISBN 13 eBook: 978-0-7684-5560-1
ISBN 13 HC: 978-0-7684-5562-5
ISBN 13 LP: 978-0-7684-5561-8

For Worldwide Distribution, Printed in the U.S.A.

7 8 / 24 23

DEDICATION

I dedicate this book to Jesus for coming to earth to make Your Father "Our Father" and for bringing us to the throne and teaching us to pray!

ACKNOWLEDGMENT

Edie Mourey, thanks for your labor with me in bringing this message forth.

CONTENTS

FOREWORD

WE LIVE IN CONFUSING AND URGENT TIMES.

Followers of Jesus face a constant barrage of cultural forces and external crisis' that threaten to derail the Church from her calling and identity. We are seeing an increase in secularism in our time that seeks with ever-increasing force to push faith and Christ out of the public square and consciousness.

We are seeing a rise in worldliness inside the Church, as things other generations viewed as sins are being recategorized as lifestyle choices. Every major Christian denomination in the United States is in serious decline, and we seem to stand by helplessly as another generation chooses to walk away from faith. One recent study found that in the next 30 years, 50 percent of the churches in the US will close, and over 42 million young people will walk away from the Church.[1]

How did it come to this? Where do we go from here? How can you and I respond as followers of Jesus with both faithfulness and fruitfulness?

---

1 https://www.greatopportunity.org

Some people believe the answer is purely theological. If we just had a more educated Church with doctrinal strength we could fend off the decline. But we have more theological training and resources than the early Church could comprehend. Will another class or seminar bring the intimacy and power we ache for?

Some believe the solution is political. We need to fight for a return to our sacred past and reclaim the highest courts and offices of our land. As good as this may be, we cannot legislate love for Jesus in the heart. We have had more political and cultural power than those in the persecuted Church could fathom and yet our love grows cold.

Other believe we need to work harder. We are simply a lazy Church. If we really poured ourselves out with renewed discipline, we could make a change. Yet the current Church has more programs and initiatives and offerings than other generations could conceive of. There are alarming rates of pastoral and volunteer burnout today.

The truth is we have not rightly diagnosed our condition, or discerned the root of the problem. We are missing both the threat and opportunity of our time. As the prophet Jeremiah lamented, "They offer superficial treatments for my people's mortal wound.[2]" The true response to the moment is first and foremost a response to a person, not a problem. We don't need more ideas about what we should do, we need deeper intimacy with the one who holds wisdom and power and knowledge in His hand.

---

2   Jeremiah 6:14 (NLT)

That's why Corey's book is so timely, and so important. Corey calls us back to the things of first importance and the true solution to the powerlessness we feel in our own lives and the Church at large. Corey has taken all he has learned in a 20-year journey of intimacy with God and has given us deep revelation from the secret place. These are not ideas or insights from the Bible, the Spirit has written these on his heart and they will bleed from the pages of this book and into your life.

Reading this book made me weep for fresh hunger for God and stirred my spirit to seek Him with a new level of desperation and intensity. This book has the potential to help you recover and the Church discover the reality and possibility of a genuine awakening in the Church and renewal in our world in these crucial days.

Indeed, like never before, may God teach us to pray.

—JON TYSON

THE SCHOOL
OF PRAYER

THE DISCIPLES SAW IT ALL. THEY WITNESSED EVERY MIRA-cle. They heard every message. They beheld every deliverance. They observed every prayer.

For three and a half years, the disciples got a front-row seat to Jesus' life. They watched God the Son talking to God the Father through God the Spirit. The One through whom everything was made—the One through whom all the worlds were formed—communed with the Father in the very presence of the disciples. And they weren't witnessing some religious activity performed by Jesus. No, prayer was His life, His inhale, His exhale.

Jesus didn't have to stir Himself in any way to start a con-versation with the Father. He simply moved from speaking words to those around Him to lifting His eyes to Heaven and talking to the Father.

Not only did the disciples see Jesus pray, they watched in awe as Jesus cast out demons with a word. They stared in disbelief as Jesus healed lepers, made the lame to walk, and caused the blind to see. They heard His masterful Sermon on the Mount and were often perplexed by His metaphors on the Kingdom of Heaven. They observed His effortless evangelism with the woman at the well. They looked on with great amazement as He brought the dead back to life. They even saw Lazarus come up out of the tomb after having been dead for four days!

Yes, the disciples were eyewitnesses to Jesus' life and ministry, yet we don't see one recorded time in Scripture where they petitioned Jesus, "Teach us to preach." We don't see one recorded time where they said, "Teach us to heal," "Teach us to prophesy," or "Teach us to do miracles." After spending three and a half years with the Son of God, they requested, *"Lord, teach us to pray"* (Luke 11:1).

At the end of the day, what the disciples wanted was Jesus' prayer life. They wanted what happened when He closed His eyes and spoke to the Father. They understood there was a way to pray, and they desperately wanted to be taught it. They had connected the dots and discovered that Jesus' public life of ministry was the direct result of His private life of prayer.

Their request has made me reevaluate my call as a leader. It has provoked me to ask Jesus to teach me to pray. It has driven my pursuit of Him over the past twenty-five years of my life. It has also caused me to ask myself, if the greatest leader of all time produced this in the ones who saw Him the most—if the greatest leader of all time came down from Heaven to Earth to teach His disciples about prayer—what am I doing? Does anyone want my prayer life?

It's time for some introspection for us all in the Body of Christ. With everything we are doing for the Kingdom, I am concerned we are *not* doing the one thing that will make all the difference, and that's modeling and teaching Jesus' life of prayer. The reason I am concerned is because prayer is the great exposer of reality. The twentieth-century revivalist Leonard Ravenhill rightfully said, "No man is greater than his prayer life."[1] We can fool people, we can wow people, but what happens when we close our eyes and open our mouths? That's the litmus test of reality that cannot be manipulated or faked.

Oh, that we all would ask, "Lord, teach us to pray."

This request has been lacking in the Church, but I believe God is stirring us as He is awakening us to the hour in which we live. I'm grateful for the messages that have told me I need to pray, but I believe we are in a new hour that requires mothers and fathers who have broken through the plastic encounter into something so real that, when they open their mouths, angels move, demons move, and hearts move!

This generation is looking for those who will take them by the hand and introduce them to the realm of Heaven and teach them how to bring it down here on Earth. We need those who will teach us how to access resources and have them manifested in our lives, in our nations, and in our generations!

The disciples understood that every other ministry Jesus manifested was the direct result of His ministry to the Father in prayer. Jesus taught them on how to access Heaven and change Earth. We need more than just instructors who teach us principles of prayer. We need messengers to impart keys to ascending into Heaven and releasing it into the earth, changing real lives and real circumstances with Heaven's resources.

RELEASING HEAVEN ON EARTH

After I got saved in 1997 as I was just entering my twenties, I spent two years with two fifty-year-old women and one eighty-year-old woman. These women taught me how to pray. They taught me about early morning prayer, late night prayer, and "praying through." They taught me not to wait on my favorite song to play before I started praying, but to take the Word of God, mingle it with communion with the Holy Spirit, and begin to declare God's Word back to Him. All of these things marked me deeply, but even more deeply than that was experiencing what I felt and what I saw when they opened their mouths: I could feel God. I got to watch them bring Heaven down to Earth.

I am grateful for their training and for much of the training of the Body of Christ in the area of prayer, but the truth is we need more of it, and we need it to rise up from the pages of books and be fleshed out in real time by mothers and fathers who don't just talk about it or preach about it, but they actually do it.

One of the greatest places this is going to happen is in our homes. I have a vision for a generation of mothers and fathers. I see their children rising in the morning and finding Mom and Dad in the living room with their Bibles open, notebooks open, pen in hand, and worship music on. I see their children looking at the faces of their parents, beholding the tears streaming down Mom's and Dad's faces as they pray to the Father in Heaven. I see those children grow with the understanding that prayer is not something done once a week at church—it's a lifestyle. I see them understanding life is all about having an ongoing, intimate relationship with a real Man named Jesus. And then I see these children pursuing Him with the same consistent burning desire as their parents.

Parents, your kids will remember your tears when you talked to Jesus far more than your words to them about following Jesus.

This, my friend, is what will produce a new breed of believers, leaders, and missionaries. That kind of prayer and relationship with God will impact the Church and the Kingdom of God like no other activity we can do.

"Teach us to pray." This is where we begin our journey toward closing the gap between where we are now in proximity and where Jesus wants to take us in intimacy. It's also the school of prayer where we learn how to ascend into Heaven so that we can release Heaven on Earth. This journey will change us, purify us, and refine us, but it will also prepare us to be conduits of Heaven in the earth.

Three years ago, while pressing into Luke 11 and the disciples' desire to be taught in prayer, I heard the Holy Spirit say to me, "Corey, I want you to join Me in teaching this generation in prayer. I want you to take the last twenty-five years of prayer and the messages they have produced, take a generation by the hand, and bring them to Me. I also want you to take the times you didn't do it right and break shame off a generation so they can come boldly to the throne of grace."

This book along with other resources and messages are my feeble attempts to give to Jesus what He longs for: His people to be a people of prayer and His house to be a house of prayer.

We've got to move from just being told to pray to giving a generation instruction on how to pray and how to pray when it's hard—when they hit the walls of failure, of shame, and of boredom.

I believe that the spirit of prayer falls on the life of prayer, so I want to show you what a life of prayer looks like, finding out where and how it is developed and lived. The Holy Spirit loves to take bored, distracted people like us, bring us to the throne room, and teach us how to access Heaven. And through our mouths and our lives, He releases Heaven into the earth. Whether you've been walking with the Lord five minutes, five years, or fifty years, I believe that this book has the potential to release a radical shift of intimacy and authority in your prayer life.

I'm done talking about it. Let's jump in!

DEVELOPING A LIFE OF PRAYER

1

AT HIS FEET

THERE IS ONE WOMAN IN THE BIBLE WHO UNDERSTOOD the importance of one thing. She understood the importance of proximity to Jesus. Her name was Mary of Bethany.

We see Mary only three times in Scripture, yet in every instance, she is at Jesus' feet (see Luke 10:38-42; John 11; 12:1-3). Somehow, she discovered the one thing that moved Jesus the most, and regardless of how unpopular it was, she gave herself to it.

Mary never had a big ministry. She never wrote her own epistle. In fact, we don't hear anything about her after her appearance in John 12. And only one statement—one line— she said is recorded in the Word of God: *"Lord, if You had been here, my brother would not have died"* (John 11:32).

Amazingly, every time we see her in the biblical text, Jesus was defending her, praising her, and calling all of us to look at her and model ourselves after her. It seems to me that this woman saw Jesus for who He was before everyone else. She saw Him, she figured out what moved Him, and she learned it. She learned His love language, and she fully threw herself into playing the strings of His heart. That's why He defended her and why He fought her battles for her. That's why, to me, she is one of the most impactful persons in the Bible outside of Jesus.

COURAGE TO SIT

It took courage to do what Mary did—to sit when her sister, Martha, was working. To sit when there was so much going on. To sit instead of "doing" for Jesus.

From the very first time we meet her in the Word, Mary was breaking through norms and expectations. She was a box breaker. She shredded protocols, systems, and expectations. She broke through into a place in Jesus that few have ever breached. She broke through busyness, distraction, and anxiety. As a matter of fact, every time we see Mary, she was breaking through something in God. More specifically, she was breaking through the swirl of activity around Jesus.

First and foremost, Mary had the courage to sit down, shut up, and cultivate a history with God, building intimacy with Jesus and His Word. She learned to wait on Him—at His feet.

Let's look more closely at our introduction to this courageous woman and her sister:

> [Jesus] *entered a certain village; and a certain woman named Martha welcomed Him into her*

house. And she had a sister called Mary, who also sat at Jesus' feet and heard His word. But Martha was distracted with much serving, and she approached Him and said, "Lord, do You not care that my sister has left me to serve alone? Therefore tell her to help me." And Jesus answered and said to her, "Martha, Martha, you are worried and troubled about many things. But one thing is needed, and Mary has chosen that good part, which will not be taken away from her" (Luke 10:38-42).

If there are four terms that characterize the current state of the Church and specifically her leaders, they would be *distracted*, *much serving*, *worried*, and *troubled*. Distraction is the rule of the day. There is so much distraction in the Church, distraction in our ministries, distraction in our workplaces, distraction in our homes. Busyness, anxiety, and demands are all around Jesus. They generate a swirl whereby everything is moving around Him, including us. And the problem this can create is—as close as we may be to Him—we never encounter Him.

Why?

Because we're caught in the swirl.

We need a new breed of people, who like Mary, refuse to worship the god of busyness. They refuse to worship the god of distraction. These people are courageous in that they refuse to miss the moment, so they choose to sit at the feet of Jesus and listen.

God wants to train us in this hour to learn how to take advantage of the moment. He wants to teach us that doing something is not what releases an eruption in the Church. It's not necessarily what releases Heaven on Earth. Waiting before Jesus, sitting at His feet, listening to Him—these are the agents that draw the power and glory of God earthward!

You don't want to miss the moment when the Son of God is in your house. If you don't learn to discover the holy moments of His presence in your house, in your car, in your bedroom, in your prayer closet, or in your workplace, you will be caught in the swirl, eddying all around Jesus, and you'll never encounter Him.

When we become so busy with the activity surrounding Jesus and do not build our lives and churches at His feet, the fruit will manifest in our comparing our situation, our position, our work, our job, our ministry to that of another, and this will lead to an accusation against Jesus. That's what happened to Martha.

"DON'T YOU CARE?"

The mistake many make when looking at Martha and Mary in Luke 10 is they try to reduce this story to Mary versus Martha, but there is so much more going on than that. It's not Mary *versus* Martha. It's Mary *before* Martha. You see, we need both. Honestly, I believe that every true Mary will become a true Martha. When you sit at His feet, you become filled with the dreams of His heart, and that puts you to work to manifest His dreams in the earth. But it's absolutely critical to find yourself at His feet, prioritizing Him over the stuff and needs around Him.

There is a divine order. There is a good part. There is a first commandment. There are first works, and Jesus is establishing this truth in this story.

Why wasn't Martha seeing it?

She was too busy, too worried, too troubled, too caught up in doing, and her eyes had fixed on what someone else wasn't doing. While not seeing the priority or value that Jesus was highlighting, she was seeing something. She was seeing her sister, Mary, and noticing that Mary was sitting at Jesus' feet, not helping her at all.

You always know you're a Martha first when all you see are Marys at His feet.

One of the biggest lessons Jesus is teaching here answers this question: Where do you find your primary reward? Will His words define you, or will what you do for Him define you?

If you make what you do for Him your primary reward, there are several things that will begin to happen in your life. You will start seeing comparison, envy, and accusation against Jesus arise within. You can see this clearly by Martha's response to Jesus: "Don't you care that my sister has left me to serve alone?" Martha was questioning Jesus' empathy and fairness.

You know you are serving in a wrong spirit when you become aware of what other people are not doing. This kind of serving will ultimately lead to accusation against Jesus concerning His empathy and fairness.

I've watched hundreds of people over the last two decades make what they do for Jesus their primary reward, and it always ends up with this growing accusation that Jesus isn't paying them enough based on how much they've worked for Him. Comparison creeps in and wholly contaminates their spiritual lives. They always feel that they aren't seen or appreciated and valued, and this leads to frustration, jealousy, envy, and anger.

Conversely, the heart rooted in intimacy is unaware of itself and unaware of everybody else in its service for Jesus. Mary didn't see Mary, and she didn't see Martha. She was just lost in Jesus. And the works born of doing the first works first result in works that last for eternity.

DIALED IN TO LISTEN

Mary did the most revolutionary thing ever. She refused to get caught up in the swirl of distraction around Jesus. She was blind to everyone and everything else but Jesus. She dialed down. She sat down. She shut up. She looked up. She listened. And she let Jesus fight her battles for her.

I believe God is raising up a new breed of people in the Body of Christ who are going to define success and impact in a different way. They won't define success in how big, how much, or how great the size of their influence is. Neither will they continue to believe the lie that says, "The busier you are, the more successful and impactful you are." Instead, success to them will be measured by the size of their hearts and present-day intimacy with God and His Word. This new breed will break agreement with the gods of busyness, distraction, and anxiety, and will prioritize minutes, hours, weeks, months, years, and decades at Jesus' feet with their Bibles open and their hearts dialed in to listen.

The most impactful point of this story is that Mary sat down and heard Jesus' words. The greatest impact we can have is when we move with Him in His timing. This is learned through waiting. Mary *"sat at Jesus' feet and heard His word"* (Luke 10:39).

I believe we've lost the power of His Word in our mouths because we've lost the power of His Word in our ears. There is a direct connection between the priority you give to hearing Him speak and the authority of your speaking for Him.

For years, I cried out to the Lord that none of my words would fall to the ground just like the prophet Samuel (see 1 Sam. 3:19). I'll never forget when the Lord told me, "Corey, how do you expect none of your words to fall to the ground when so many of My words fall to the ground of your heart?"

In that moment, I realized God honors the words of His servants to the same degree that His servants honor His words.

When our lives and ministries are built more around busyness and managing opportunities than sitting at His feet and hearing His words, the words we speak and sing—no matter how biblical they are—do not carry the same weight and authority to shift people, change circumstances, and impact nations. They can't and don't release Heaven here on Earth.

We desperately need words that have been received in the furnace of silence and solitude at His feet. His words always break out of the silence, and we must begin to prioritize hearing those words. Then, because we have sat at His feet and listened to Him, His words that we deliver to others will have power. Our spending time listening to Jesus' words will restore power to those words as we deliver them. They will have life and impact on the hearers.

My greatest fear about the day when I stand before Jesus and He then applies fire to my life's work is that I find out that what took me sixty years to build is consumed in six milliseconds. Think of that—sixty years in six milliseconds!

I want to invest the best of my strength, energy, and time at a place that Jesus esteems and calls the *good part*.

Why?

Because He said that part *"will not be taken away"* (Luke 10:42).

NOT TAKEN AWAY

Mary simply invested the most valuable commodity—her time—into eternity. She took the window of opportunity and sowed her time into eternity, and it will last forever. She sowed into a place where moth and rust cannot destroy (see Matt. 6:19-21). She sowed into a place unseen by man, and it resulted in eternal treasure.

We've graduated thousands of ministers from our seminaries, but are these men and women being trained in the lost art of waiting on God? Where are the priests who burn before God in empty rooms and have discovered the beauty of God, the mind of God, the ways of God, and when they speak of Him, they don't regurgitate something they read in a book but speak from the mount of divine vision?

The kingdom was stripped from King Saul and given to a *"man after God's own heart"* when Saul was driven by the demands of the people and, out of fear of losing them, felt compelled to act and didn't wait on God (1 Sam. 15; Acts 13:21-22).

There is nothing more subtly deceptive in the Christian experience than the slow removal of the one thing and of its being first place, first priority, in your life. Another subtle deception is that it's not that big of a deal. The devil will let you do a lot, but if you want to put hell on notice, take your seat at Jesus' feet and don't let any amount of money, platform, opportunity, betrayal, hardship, or tribulation talk you out of that.

The Lord told me years ago, "Corey, if you go after one thing, you will get everything. But if you go after everything, you will get nothing."

How do we come out of the whirlwind of activity, Instagram, Facebook, Snapchat, TikTok, YouTube, open doors, and opportunities, and build a life of hearing His words?

In the simplest terms, it means making a time and place sacred and consistent, where you meet with God and it's just you, Him, and your Bible. This one decision will dramatically alter everything in your life, and the enemy understands this more than most believers do.

A life at Jesus' feet looks like sitting long enough until all the other voices, inside and out, are drowned out. As soon as you get serious about this, every distraction under the sun will surface in your mind and emotions. Fantasies, seductions, and lusts of being richer, more successful, or more connected will emerge. Fears, insecurities, and lies will manifest. Just stay at His feet.

As you sit before the flame of His Word and Spirit, the dross will rise. Pay no attention to it. Just stay there.

Your mind will wander every three minutes, and you will quickly come up with things to do, people to see, and errands to run. Just write them down and keep looking at Him.

Facebook, Instagram, Snapchat, Twitter, texts, e-mails, and videos will scream for you to see them, respond to them, and engage with them, but you can go for five more minutes. Just put your phone down and stay a little longer.

Boredom will settle in, and you will feel so raw as your bored heart comes into a realization that God isn't as beautiful as you thought, and it's just raw you and raw Him. Don't be afraid of the boredom because, on the other side of the boredom, is a realm of fascination and glory that you will never get over. Just keep slowly reading that Bible and whispering it aloud until you see Him and hear Him.

Do whatever you have to do. Rock back and forth, pace back and forth, until you hear. Sing until you hear. Sit in silence until you hear. Just stay five more minutes.

The taskmaster within will begin to tell you to quit being lazy and do something more productive with your time, your gifts, and your abilities, but don't listen to the taskmaster. Just stay a little longer. His voice will leave. I promise you.

Some voices will remind you of what you've done, even last night. They will whisper that you're not worthy and could never be forgiven. They are lies. Just stay five more minutes.

When shame makes you want to hide from Him, sit at His feet and declare over yourself: "By Your blood, I'm clean, I'm righteous, and I'm blameless in Your sight." Just keep declaring that and receive.

Other voices will condemn you because you're not doing enough in regard to prayer. They will say you need to be more radical and more disciplined. Just take a deep breath and receive the Father's full pleasure right now. There is nothing more you need to do. You are freely and fully loved, right now.

There will be voices from without where people need you to fix their problems, pray with them, talk to them, counsel them. Just tell them, "Five more minutes."

These are only a few of the distractions, worry, and anxiety that surround sitting at His feet and hearing His Word. I promise you that, if you make this the priority and stay a little longer, you will discover life like you never have experienced it before.

"ONE THING IS NEEDED"

In the Kingdom, there are first things, first works, and a first commandment. The Bible tells us that, if we do the first things first, it will affect everything else we do. There is one thing needed. There is a good part. There are first works. There is a seeking first. David chose the one thing in Psalm 27:4. Paul chose it in Philippians 3:13-14, and Jesus is calling you to choose it today.

When you first read "one thing is needed," you can think to yourself, *How can only one thing be needed?* Many things are needed. There are many aspects of the Christian life—of our own lives, our families, our marriages, and our kids. What does it mean for one thing to be needed?

When asking the Lord about this, I felt like He told me, "Corey, you need to understand that there is one decision, there is a one thing, and if you do this one thing, it will set a trajectory for many other things to be aligned in your life. If, however, you don't get that one thing right, it will take you in a completely different direction. You can have the whole world yet lose your soul."

If Jesus, the Son of God, highlights one thing that is needed above everything else, why aren't we hearing much about this or seeing it modeled? Our silence on this issue is setting us up for dramatic exposure in the coming days.

I'm convinced that the present-day Church and its leadership are simply not equipped internally to handle what is coming externally—it's fire! It's the glory of God and the shaking of everything that can be shaken.

God is driving His people into deeper intimacy with Him and into deeper intimacy with one another. He's going to release great presence and great pressure on the whole globe to deliver us from our own ingenuity, our own wisdom, our own abilities, and our own thoughts while driving us into greater humility, mission, and unity with the Holy Spirit. He's going to release great presence and great pressure.

Why?

Because presence and pressure produce prayer. And in prayer at the feet of Jesus, listening to His words, is where He is going to develop the life of prayer anointed by the spirit of prayer.

We only unify with that which we submit to. We only unify with the Holy Spirit to the degree that we submit to the Holy Spirit.

Because we have falsely concluded that success is solely found in how big, how much, and how many versus the current size of our hearts and present-day intimacy with Jesus and each other, we aren't prepared to navigate the coming dynamics.

We must draw close to God and each other to navigate these days because they won't get any easier than today. As the Lord told the prophet Jeremiah, *"If you have run with the footmen, and they have wearied you, then how can you contend with horses?"* (Jer. 12:5).

In today's language, how are we going to handle a ten on our treadmills when the two is wearing us out?

YOU MUST CHOOSE

Jesus said, *"Mary has chosen that good part, which will not be taken away from her"* (Luke 10:42).

So, what did Mary do?

Mary chose. She had a choice. Jesus did not make the choice for her. Neither will He make it for you but will honor the choice you make.

I believe God is offering one of the greatest choices to you in this hour. Can you—in the midst of all the allurements, voices, seductions, opportunities, and money—choose to sit at His feet with a Bible open and an engaged heart, listening to His voice?

It's one thing to sit at His feet when you have no options, but what about when you live in a nation that is filled with options? Who can do it in the big cities? God is calling for a people out of Dallas, Los Angeles, Atlanta, San Francisco, New York City, Tokyo, London, Rio de Janeiro, Buenos Aires, Nairobi, and every other city in the world who can begin to declare war on the seduction of busyness by dialing down and listening. He's also calling people in little towns and communities from all the countries of the world to come out of boredom and to discover fascination with Him, our beautiful God.

Jesus made a profound statement in Luke 10. In essence, He said what this girl did—her refusing to get caught in the swirl around Him and choosing instead to look at Him and listen to Him—will live forever. Mary took her greatest commodity—time—and sowed it into a place where moth and rust cannot destroy. What she did will NEVER be taken away from her. Eternal treasures. Eternal investments. This is the stuff I'm going after. I want the stuff that will live forever. I want the stuff that will endure the fire of His gaze and be carried with me into eternity as gold, silver, and precious stones, don't you?

I'll never forget hearing a teaching from Leonard Ravenhill on First Corinthians 3. He spoke on how the eternal fire of God will be applied to our works here in the earth to see whether they were done for God or for ourselves. Here's the portion of Scripture Ravenhill was preaching from:

> *Now if anyone builds on this foundation with gold, silver, precious stones, wood, hay, straw, each one's work will become clear; for the Day will declare it, because it will be revealed by fire; and the fire will test each one's work, of what sort it is. If anyone's work which he has built on it endures, he will receive a reward. If anyone's work is burned, he will suffer loss; but he himself will be saved, yet so as through fire* (1 Corinthians 3:12-15).

In this message, Ravenhill highlighted the difference between the gold, silver, and precious stones *and* the wood, hay, and straw. He stated that you find the gold, silver, and precious stones under the ground, hidden from the eyes of men, while you find the other three above the ground where everyone can see.[2]

We are going to be utterly shocked at the judgment seat when we find the stuff that everyone saw in this age isn't as beautiful with the eyes of eternity, yet the stuff that was hidden from the eyes of men and known only to God will translate to gold, silver, and precious stones that we will carry with us into the age to come.

I want to be like Mary who did something that will never be taken away, something that will live forever; therefore, I am choosing to sit at Jesus' feet, dial in, and listen to His words because it's from this place my life will have its greatest impact, and it's from here the lifestyle of prayer is developed.

2

IN THE WILDERNESS

THERE WAS MAN WHOM JESUS CALLED THE GREATEST man born of a woman. His name was John the Baptist, and he lived his entire life in one place: the wilderness. Though this man never performed a miracle, never opened a blind eye, never unstopped a deaf ear, and never raised a dead person from the grave, His life and message literally shook a nation.

When most of us think of a wilderness, we think of it as the tough, dry season we have to go through so we can get to our destiny, but what if the wilderness is where we are called to live while on this earthly pilgrimage?

The wilderness that I'm talking about is not a geographical wilderness but an intentional life of choosing to live dependent on God. Nowhere is this more practically realized than through living a life of consistent prayer for decades.

One of the greatest reasons, however, that many do not persist for decades in prayer is because of our disdain for weakness. And yet, it's in our weakness that His strength is made perfect. Prayer will inevitably bring you into your need for God, and this is absolutely beautiful. This is what Jesus called *blessed,* and yet we live in a culture that does everything in its power to insulate us from dependence. We live in a society that only values bigger, better, and more, and yet Jesus, who was fully God, emptied Himself of all of His divine privilege, came to the earth, and lived dependent upon Abba as His Source.

When we are asking Jesus to teach us to pray, we are asking Him to make us humble as He is humble, and that strikes at the heart of our independence and self-determination.

We must face the truth about prayer. It is powerful yet beggarly at its core. The essential revelation of prayer is that God is strong when we are weak, and few things speak of weakness like taking our time, looking at an invisible God, and relying on Him as our Source.

Most of us view the wilderness as the thing we endure and get through on our way to our Promised Land, but what if God is calling us to a life in the wilderness? What if He is calling you to receive your destiny or have it manifest there?

I have watched countless people give themselves to prayer for weeks, months, and sometimes a few years even. Somewhere along the way, though, they shift out of the life of prayer as Jesus goes from wooing them to confronting them.

One of the main things Jesus confronts is our wrong paradigm of prayer. Many of us are guilty of praying as long as there is a benefit for us on the back end. We will "put in our time" with God as long as it results in more opportunities, more anointing, more money, and more stuff. God will kill this in us in the school of prayer because Jesus isn't a stepladder into our destiny. He wants to kill our destiny so that He can release His destiny through us.

So, Jesus takes us to the wilderness. This is where God brings His favorite ones because He longs for greater intimacy and union with us. In the same way He delivered Israel out of Egypt so that He could bring them to the wilderness to marry them, God is bringing a whole generation out of the shallow end of Christianity into a deeper life of prayer and consecration. These will be forerunners like John the Baptist who spend their lives in the wilderness, praying and fasting and preparing for the coming of the Lord.

JOHN THE BAPTIST

The last recorded words of Malachi promised:

> *Behold, I will send you Elijah the prophet before the coming of the great and dreadful day of the Lord. And he will turn the hearts of the fathers to the children, and the hearts of the children to the fathers, lest I come and strike the earth with a curse* (Malachi 4:5-6).

God said He was going to send Elijah to Israel, yet there were four hundred years of silence with no Elijah in sight after He spoke the promise through the prophet Malachi. The Old Testament closed. Century after century followed, and each generation waited and prayed for the prophet *and* the

Consolation of Israel to appear. No doubt, there were intercessors like Anna and Simeon who were crying out to God for the fulfillment to happen in their generation.

One day, it was Zacharias's turn to burn incense in the temple. While performing his priestly service, the angel Gabriel appeared to him and said, *"Do not be afraid, Zacharias, for your prayer is heard; and your wife Elizabeth will bear you a son, and you shall call his name John"* (Luke 1:13).

In one moment, the prayer that had been growing for decades and the cry to break off barrenness from his and his wife's lives were answered. In that answer, the cry from generations to break off the gentile domination and the oppression over the nation of Israel seemed so much closer to being satisfied.

Gabriel continued,

> *And you will have joy and gladness, and many will rejoice at his birth. For he will be great in the sight of the Lord, and shall drink neither wine nor strong drink. He will also be filled with the Holy Spirit, even from his mother's womb. And he will turn many of the children of Israel to the Lord their God. He will also go before Him in the spirit and power of Elijah "to turn the hearts of the father to the children," and the disobedient to the wisdom of the just, to make ready a people prepared for the Lord"* (Luke 1:14-17).

There it was—the announcement that the forerunner, the one with the Malachi 4 anointing, was coming! After four hundred years of silence, Gabriel showed up and basically reiterated what God had said through Malachi those centuries before, "Elijah is coming!"

And so, John the Baptist was birthed out of the wilderness of his parents' barrenness and then began to grow strong in spirit. Luke 1:80 then tells us, he *"was in the deserts till the day of his manifestation to Israel."*

John was out in the wilderness for twenty years, living among a radical group of people who were given to prayer, fasting, and eating the Word together. What happened to John in the wilderness over those twenty years?

All of his illusions were destroyed. All of his fantasies were destroyed. All of his props were destroyed. All of his masks were destroyed. All of the tentacles of the culture were ripped out of his soul, and he was brought into an entirely different realm. He completely detoxed from the culture of his day.

I cannot overstate that, if you are going to persist in a life of prayer, you will come face to face with all the illusions within, the imposters within, and you will come into an earth-shattering revelation of God and yourself, thereby delivering you from the voices in and out of the Church that say, "Bigger, better, more is best." This message is so hollow and doesn't have the power truly to deliver people from the spirit of this age.

John the Baptist lived in the wilderness waiting—eating Genesis, Exodus, Leviticus, Numbers, and Deuteronomy.

He was getting lost in the Psalms, Isaiah, Ezekiel, Daniel, Zechariah, and Malachi. The words in these books became more than Bible verses he memorized or familiarized himself with. He was devouring these books. The words within them were being imparted to him.

In Deuteronomy 8, the Lord told Moses that He brought the children of Israel into the wilderness to test them, humble them, and make them know that man doesn't live by bread but by every word that comes out of the mouth of God. This is what happens in the wilderness. He makes you live on His words.

After twenty years of eating His words, the Word came to John, and all of history was changed: *"The word of God came to John the son of Zacharias in the wilderness"* (Luke 3:2).

What do you think that looked like?

John baptized an entire generation in the waters of the Jordan, preparing them for the coming of the Messiah. He called to them to change course, to repent. He invited them to come out of their sin and come into the Kingdom of Heaven.

John the Baptist was fearless. He lived by a completely different set of values and a radical system. Where did he get them?

He got them in the wilderness. In fact, he never left the wilderness. And it was his voice *"crying in the wilderness"* that proclaimed, *"Prepare the way of the Lord; make His paths straight"* (Matt. 3:3).

THE MAKING OF A VOICE

God called me into full-time ministry in the weakest and most vulnerable season of my life. I was the most disqualified, and yet God in His grace qualified me.

It was May 1998, and I was living in Arkansas. I was twenty-one years old and recently engaged to Dana, now my wife of over twenty years. The first year of my salvation was marked by a move of God that swept through my hometown. We saw half of the high school saved, and a local church began to hold four to five meetings a week to host the presence of God. We saw many salvations, deliverances, healings, and times of refreshing by the Holy Spirit.

Earlier in the year, God had begun to turn my heart toward Dana who had been leading young people in the church and was also an anointed singer. One thing led to another, and before we knew it, we wanted to get married. Everything happened very fast, and honestly, we didn't have proper accountability and discipleship regarding boundaries. Sadly, we crossed a lot of them. This was absolutely devastating to us because we loved God deeply and wanted to please Him, yet we were still very immature in many ways.

In the middle of this season, a friend encouraged me to attend a conference in Kansas City called, "Friends of the Bridegroom Conference." In so many ways, I felt completely disqualified from ever being used by God. I don't remember a lot from that weekend, but I do remember that Isaiah 40 was the main passage used throughout my time there—*"The voice of one crying out in the wilderness, 'Prepare the Way of the*

Lord.'" One preacher declared that God was raising up voices across the earth like that of John the Baptist's who would prepare the Church and the lost for the second coming of Jesus. Through the lives and message of these voices, they would prepare others for His glory and shaking.

Isaiah 40 was ultimately God's message to a completely shattered and hopeless people who had lost connection to the promises of God. It was a message to people who had lost faith, yet God encouraged them that He who made and kept His promises to Abraham, Isaac, and Jacob would fulfill every word He had spoken no matter how much it looked like His words weren't coming to pass.

As I listened to the preacher in Kansas City, I was struck to the heart for three days by two sentences: "I don't want to be an echo. I want to be a voice." These lines just kept going over and over and over inside me. As I said them aloud, I knew that I wanted to be a voice in my generation, not merely an echo of somebody else's message or some other cool thing that I had heard. I wanted something so real in God that, when I spoke about Him, angels would move, devils would move, and the hearts of men and women would move!

Don't get me wrong. I was grateful for others who were a voice. It's simply that I was not satisfied to rejoice merely in their light while never getting the reality for myself. I knew God was calling me to more than "just dancing around someone else's fire." He was calling me to get *into* the fire.

Something told me then that it wouldn't come cheaply— that there was a place where voices were formed. Yes, it's the wilderness. In the same way John went to the desert praying, fasting, and eating the Word for decades, I grew to understand that God was calling me to an intense life of preparation and consecration. It would require a deep devouring of the Word of God so that, in a coming day, I would manifest the nature of Christ through my life and words. This kind of authority in preaching would be fleshed out in my life as the Word becomes flesh in us.

In the same way that an electrician runs the electrical wiring through small holes to wire a house, I knew God wanted to take me on a guided tour from Genesis to Revelation, revealing His Son in Me and through Me, so that I would be entrusted with the deep mysteries of Christ. I knew that my part was to prepare for the wiring, but I also knew that there would be a day of manifestation when the light switch was turned on and that which had been prepared was ready to be a conduit of the power, glory, and conviction of the Holy Spirit.

Also, during this time, the words of Leonard Ravenhill resounded in my being: "A sermon born in the head reaches the head; a sermon born in the heart reaches the heart."[3]

I was called into the ministry at this conference. In the weakest and most vulnerable time of my life, God called me. He spoke comfort to my heart, breaking the power of the enemy off me and reconnecting me to His storyline for my life.

It's been over twenty years since that conference, and I could have never imagined the journey the Lord would take me and my family on. These years have been filled with countless hours in prayer, where Holy Spirit has cried through me, groaned through me, and prayed through me. Entire chapters from the Word have been written on my heart as the Spirit of Revelation has rested on me for days, weeks, months, and even years. Many nights, I have been awakened by God and had Him download His heart to me. Other days, the Spirit has rested on me in a burning fashion so that all I could do was weep.

There have been many other times, however, that have been pretty boring and uninspiring as I have sat for weeks asking God to speak to me and have heard nothing. In the same places where I've been caught up in the Spirit, I've fallen asleep out of weariness and boredom. Truth be told, there have been days when I haven't even felt saved!

In all of these seasons, my insecurities, fears, and wrong paradigms of God and myself were clearly manifested in me and to others. I have walked through times when I came face to face with my own brokenness, weakness, and sin. On such occasions, feeling completely naked and ashamed, I've heard God say to me out of His great grace, mercy, and love, "You are My son in whom I'm well pleased."

This is what the wilderness looks like.

The wilderness is the furnace of transformation. It's the context by which God causes all the dross, all the culture, and all its stuff to surface. We get delivered from the masks and the illusions, and we begin to see correctly.

It's in the wilderness where voices are formed. If God has truly called you into ministry, He will prepare you in the wilderness. If He has called you to follow Him, He will take you to the wilderness.

It's in the wilderness where all of the props are kicked out—where we are humbled, stripped, and made to know that man does *"not live by bread alone"* but *"by every word that proceeds out from the mouth of the Lord"* (Deut. 8:3).

It's in the wilderness where God deconstructs everything you thought you knew about Him, and He begins to reintroduce you to Himself through the Spirit of Revelation. It's here where the knowledge of God is imparted in us (see Isa. 40:21-23).

It's in the wilderness where He takes the names of other lovers out of our hearts and mouths, and we come into the revelation that God is our Bridegroom. It's here where the revelation of our sonship gets rooted and grounded in us. It's here where His voice becomes the loudest, the strongest, and it drowns out all the other voices, seductions, and allurements of this age (see Hos. 2).

It's in the wilderness where Jesus backs you into a corner and lays hold of you and wrestles with you, changing your name and identity, and bringing you into an encounter with Him (see Gen. 32).

It's in the wilderness where you become vulnerable to God, where you receive a revelation of your smallness and of your sinfulness.

It's in the wilderness where you have an Isaiah 6 encounter. You receive a revelation of Jesus that releases repentance in you, resulting in the religious systems and constraints being cast away from you. It's here where you get delivered from a man-pleasing spirit. You then can come into *the* Man, Christ Jesus!

Voices are formed in the wilderness.

Voices never "graduate" from the wilderness.

Voices become voices through silence and solitude, and it's this quality of messenger and message that penetrates the noise of a chaotic culture in the world and in the Church. One of the reasons I've written this book is to see the restoration of voices in the Church. We are in an urgent hour, and the greatest need is voices that emerge from silence to cut through the chaos of noise.

These voices aren't motivated through networking, connecting, and building their profile. They're motivated to encounter the Voice.

These voices aren't into controlling and owning those God has entrusted to them, but whose joy is connecting them to Him. These voices are freed to get out of the way as He increases in their midst. They don't continually make themselves the center but are freed to decrease as He increases (see John 3:30).

They're not into self-worship. They don't see Jesus as serving them. These voices don't say, "I'll pay my dues. I'll do a little fasting. I'll do a little praying as long as He anoints me and fulfills all my dreams." No, these voices know it's not about them. It's all about their beautiful Lord and Savior.

Voices become voices through the Voice breaking into their shattered places. Isaiah 40 is God's voice to His people who have been shattered, whittled down, backed into a corner—those who have lost connection with His promises. I'm convinced that the global voice that will emerge in the nations toward Jerusalem in her darkest hour will be voices who have had His voice show up to them in their devastating seasons. It's only with the comfort they have received that they will be able to comfort others in the coming days (see 2 Cor. 1:4).

God is raising up voices who will feed people on the knowledge and understanding of Him. These messengers don't just have a message, but they *are* the message. Jesus, in Matthew 11:9, said that John the Baptist was *"more than a prophet."* His very life made a bigger statement than the words he spoke.

This happens when the Word has become flesh in those voices, and they carry His heart with His Word. They are shepherds who have been formed and fashioned in a specific seminary: the seminary of His heart.

As He entwines our hearts with His, we are entrusted with the deep mysteries of God and are anointed to feed others on Him. The seminary of His heart is found in the place of prayer while we are on our knees and our Bibles and hearts are open. In this seminary, we hunger to encounter the true and living God.

Before God does anything *through* His messengers, He must first do it *in* His messengers. He must first bring us to the wilderness. It's here where He starves out all of the other voices of identity, success, and greatness by continually declaring His love, beauty, and affection over us until we believe Him. The ones who receive this from Him will declare it. These will cry out, preparing the way of the Lord.

MAKING STRAIGHT

I believe that God is raising up *"shepherds according to* [His] *heart, who will feed* [people] *with knowledge and understanding"* of Him (Jer. 3:15). These will be shepherds who have been formed and fashioned in the wilderness.

I'm greatly burdened for this generation of worship leaders, pastors, preachers, and leaders in the Church. In an hour where our worship leaders and communicators are the most polished, the most educated, the most articulate, and the most attractive, there is a painful gap that I'm seeing between the *excellence* of the presentation and the *shallowness* of the presentation. Yes, you read that right. I said *presentation* twice. It's possible to say something and say nothing at the same time, and I believe we in the American Church have become professionals at it. I know there are exceptions to this generalization, but I've thought on this statement for twenty years and have seen it firsthand as I've traveled thirty-five weekends a year for the last fifteen years. I've also seen it in my own life and the lives of my friends.

How can we say all the right things, sing all the right things, yet nothing of eternity be imparted to those who hear us?

I'm afraid that, after all of our Sunday services have ended and everyone has gone home, what most of us just experienced was more of a pep rally than an encounter with the living God.

We are in desperate need of leaders who have been forged in the fires of prayer, fasting, and the Word, and out of that place, they lead the Body of Christ.

How can we once again see a recovery of apostolic messages that carry apostolic conviction, vision, and power coming out of apostolic men and women? What are those ancient paths Jeremiah 6:16 says that, if we found them, we would find rest for our souls?

I believe with all my heart that we are moving into the most spoken of generation in the Word of God, and it's the generation of the coming of our Lord Jesus Christ. These days will involve great glory, awesome presence, as well as great terror and shaking as Jesus the Judge begins to release justice in the nations. I'm afraid that the current "run-of-the-mill" training of our preachers and ministers is not enough to navigate the days ahead.

We need men and women who are on fire. Just like the seraphim—those "burning ones" around the throne of God—we need men and women who have built their lives around gazing and beholding the burning God and are thereby set aflame.

We need leaders who pray more than talk. We need leaders who have learned the lost art of waiting on God and making ministry to Him their first ministry.

We need a generation to arise who believe in revival. We need leaders who desire and foster sovereign seasons when God openly displays the rule and reign of Jesus by the outpouring of the Holy Spirit and the power and conviction of apostolic preaching.

We need shepherds who are moved by eternity. We need shepherds who are not moved by how many likes they have on their social media platforms or YouTube videos but by Heaven's smile upon them.

We need leaders who are the same in public as they are in secret. We need leaders who have concluded that encountering God in the secret place is greater than anything this world has to offer and that what they look at, listen to, talk about, and do when no one is watching are tightly bound in the Spirit of God.

We need messengers who walk with a limp. We need men and women who, like Jacob, have wrestled with the Lord through difficult circumstances and have come through leaning on Him.

We need mothers and fathers who are driven by compassion—mothers and fathers who see with God's eyes, feel with His heart, and move in His timing.

We need leaders who fear God more than man. We need leaders who believe God's opinion of them is greater than anything else.

We need preachers who know and love the Bible. The Church is in a famine of the Word, and we must have a revival of biblical preaching that restores honor to the Word of God and equips the saints in love and honor for the Word of God.

We need a generation that is full of the Holy Spirit and that loves Him deeply.

We need leaders who are hungry, always grateful, yet never satisfied.

We need shepherds who are tender and filled with mercy because they've discovered Him to be merciful with them in their most vulnerable places.

We need messengers who cry out, "Repent! The Kingdom of Heaven is at hand! The King is coming! Repent! Make straight the path."

I believe with all my heart that you are holding this book in your hands because God intends for you to be the answer to the growing crisis of leadership in the earth. Right now, just put the book down, open your hands, and whisper this prayer:

> *God, make me a voice in this generation. God, make me a shepherd after Your own heart. I want to know You for real. I want to burn with Your holy fire. I want to feel what You feel, see how You see, and move like You move. I open my heart to You. Release upon me the Spirit of Wisdom and Revelation in the knowledge of Your Son. Set my heart on fire. Lord, make my life a life of prayer. Amen.*

3

"TEACH US TO PRAY"

AS I READ THE GOSPELS AND NOTE HOW OFTEN JESUS prayed, how much He spoke on prayer, and how much He taught on prayer, I'm convinced that this left the greatest impact on His disciples once He returned to the Father.

For three and a half years, these men got a front-row seat to the life of the Son of God, and they saw Him 24/7. They saw Him early in the morning and late at night. They were in every revival service every day. Then they got to spend every evening with Him, talking about the revival service as they ate dinner.

The Gospel of John tells us there were many things Jesus did that, *"if they were written one by one,"* then *"even the world itself could not contain the books that would be written"* (21:25). And the disciples experienced them all!

The disciples got to watch Jesus pray. As I said in the introduction, they got to watch God the Son talking to God the Father through God the Spirit. And the conversation of the Godhead didn't smack of the awkwardness that the disciples' own conversations with the Son of God did.

Can you picture the way Jesus looked to the Father, the ease and freedom with which He spoke to the Father?

What did the intimacy, vulnerability, joy, honesty, humility, majesty, and revelation by which Jesus prayed look and sound like?

Can you imagine watching the One who had been with the Father from eternity past looking at the Father and talking to Him right in front of your eyes? (That thought alone is worth hours of meditation!)

Jesus could move from talking with the disciples to talking with the Father with ease and without a glitch because He lived in the bosom of the Father and never left it. Jesus lived in complete dependence on the Father. As He attested Himself,

> *The Son can do nothing of Himself, but what He sees the Father do; for whatever He does, the Son also does in like manner* (John 5:19).
>
> *I can of Myself do nothing. As I hear, I judge; and My judgment is righteous, because I do not seek My own will but the will of the Father who sent Me* (v. 30).

From Jesus' baptism to His death, He was praying. He prayed in joy, grief, sorrow, and suffering. He was constantly looking up. One time, I counted and found close to 175 verses where Jesus either was praying or teaching on prayer. Evidently, prayer wasn't a side ministry for Him. No, it was the very bone and marrow of His life. From His first message to His last, Jesus emphasized and prioritized prayer. Scripture says:

> *He Himself often withdrew into the wilderness and prayed* (Luke 5:16).
>
> *Now in the morning, having risen a long while before daylight, He went out and departed to a solitary place, and there He prayed* (Mark 1:35).
>
> *Who, in the days of His flesh, when He had offered up prayers and supplications, with vehement cries and tears to Him who was able to save Him from death, and was heard because of His godly fear* (Hebrews 5:7).
>
> *In that hour Jesus rejoiced in the Spirit and said, "I thank You, Father, Lord of heaven and earth, that You have hidden these things from the wise and prudent and revealed them to babes. Even so, Father, for so it seemed good in Your sight"* (Luke 10:21).
>
> *And Jesus lifted up His eyes and said, "Father, I thank You that You have heard Me. And I know that You always hear Me"* (John 11:41-42).
>
> *"In the world you will have tribulation; but be of good cheer, I have overcome the world." Jesus spoke these words, lifted up His eyes to heaven and said, "Father, the hour has come. Glorify Your Son, that Your Son may glorify You"* (John 16:33-17:1).

Jesus allowed His disciples to watch Him pray because He wanted them to watch Him engage with the Father in Heaven. During His time with His disciples, Jesus pulled back the curtain and provoked them by letting them see how He communed with Heaven. It undoubtedly left a lasting impression on them to see Jesus rise a *"long while before daylight"* and go to a solitary place and pray, or to watch Him make unconventional decisions like going *"through Samaria"* instead of around it as we're told He did in John 4:4. The disciples would have witnessed His decision to depart to the next city right when the city He was in presently was experiencing revival.

After seeing all Jesus said or did, what the disciples wanted was His private life of prayer. So, when Jesus had finished praying one day, they said, *"Lord, teach us to pray, as John taught his disciples"* (Luke 11:1). They understood there was a way to pray, and they desperately wanted to be taught it.

We know we need to pray. We've been told all of our Christian lives of the importance of prayer and what happens when we don't pray. Yet, somehow, that's not enough to motivate us to pray and keep praying through every season. The disciples asked Jesus to take them by the hand, as it were, and connect them with the interaction He had with Heaven.

As I consider Jesus' model of inviting His disciples to watch Him pray, I'm convinced that the Lord wants to raise up a generation to come out of their prayer closets and begin to lead corporate prayer meetings where others can watch up close and personal how to engage with God. Oh, that their prayer lives would inspire disciples to say, "I want to know

God like you. I want to talk to God the way you talk to God!" I believe God wants to raise up spiritual fathers and mothers in this generation who embody prayer and can teach it to those around them.

But here's the thing: We can only take people to where we've been or where we are currently. You can't introduce others to the realities of Heaven if you aren't living in them yourself. The disciples understood this. So, they said, *"Teach us to pray."* And that's what we must do to foster the spirit of prayer that God wants to rest on us.

"WHEN YOU PRAY"

In Luke 11, Jesus highlighted two truths about prayer. The first is found in what we call the *Lord's Prayer*, and that truth is prayer is about walking through the open door. The second truth is found in the parable that immediately follows the Lord's Prayer. In it, we discover prayer is also staying long enough for closed doors to open.

Let's look first at the Lord's Prayer. Jesus said,

> *When you pray, say: "Our Father in heaven, hallowed be Your name. Your kingdom come. Your will be done on earth as it is in heaven. Give us day by day our daily bread. And forgive us our sins, for we also forgive everyone who is indebted to us. And do not lead us into temptation, but deliver us from the evil one"* (Luke 11:2-4).

Note Jesus' first statement in His answer: *"When you pray."* He didn't say, "When you read a book or go to a conference or hear a teaching." He said, *"When you pray,"* which means you learn how to pray by praying. It also means He expects us to pray.

Prayer is on-the-job training, and you grow by doing it. Typically, we want to get all of the understanding about something before we start it. When it comes to prayer, I always tell people to start, and the Holy Spirit will begin to teach them as they pray.

Again, as I've said before, just make a consistent time and place to pray. Then show up and start reaching for God. It's truly that simple. If you build it, He will come, but if you want to get it perfect before showing up, you will never pray.

In the first line of the Lord's Prayer, Jesus emphasized the most important realities in developing your prayer life—namely, how you view God is everything.

The first line turns every thought about prayer on its head: Prayer isn't first about getting stuff. It's not about your "making a list and checking it twice." Prayer starts with answering these questions: Who are you talking to? Where does He live? And what is He like?

When most believers think of prayer, they think of that list, but Jesus thought first of a Person and then a place.

I always picture Jesus looking at me and saying, "OK, you want to learn about prayer? Write down your prayer list of everything you need Me to fix in your life."

In my imagination, I go ahead and write down my list. It reads something like this, "Save Uncle Johnny and Aunt Suzie. I need money. Deliver Grandpa Bob. Heal Grandma Barbara. I need money. Help Neighbor Johnson with his lawnmower. Did I tell You I need money?" I then hand the list to Jesus, thinking I've done what He's asked and am ready to start praying.

Now, guess what I see Him doing in my imagination?

He slowly rips up the list until it's completely shredded. Bet you didn't see that coming!

I then hear Him in my imagination say, "I want to introduce you to Someone. He's the most beautiful, the most exhilarating, the most fascinating, the most glorious Person you will ever meet. I've come to reveal Him to you.

"So, your first lesson in prayer is, when you think *prayer,* you think *list,* but I think *Person.* I want to introduce you to a Person, a place, and the Person's name. It's 'Our Father in heaven, by the way.'"

By the first line in the Lord's Prayer, we see that Jesus came to share His Father with the whole earth. He came to reveal the most glorious, kind, righteous, just, powerful, wise, loving, gentle, zealous Person who has ever been, and we get to call Him, *"Abba"* (Rom. 8:15; Gal. 4:6).

Jesus takes us to the throne and connects us with Abba Father as the foundation to all prayer. The Father's house is the house of prayer, and the revelation of the Father is the first and primary lesson in growing in prayer.

I cannot emphasize enough the importance of our knowledge of God, not only as it relates to prayer, but to the whole of Christian life. We must ask ourselves:

- What do I think of when I think of God?
- Who do I think I'm talking to when I pray?
- What's God like?
- How does God feel?

The answers to these questions reveal our paradigm or view of the Father. Do we find Him lovely? Do we enjoy Him? Do we know He enjoys us? Do we know the pleasure He takes when He looks at us?

ENCOUNTERING THE FATHER

We call Him *Father.* Prayer doesn't begin with anxiety over our separation but begins with a great exhale of "Thank You, Abba, that we are Your children and that we belong here with You." We say, "Abba, we belong to You. Abba, we are Yours. You are our Father."

We need to remind ourselves just who it is we're talking to. Let's look at Him for a moment:

- Our Father is Creator, Sustainer, and Upholder (see Ps. 55:22; Heb. 1:3; 1 Pet. 4:19).
- He is an inexhaustible treasure house of all goodness, love, wisdom, righteousness, and

power (see Ps. 33:5; 45:6; 62:11; Eccl. 2:26; Eph. 2:4).

- He is infinite, limitless, without bounds or restrictions.

- He is uncreated (see Ps. 90:2).

- He is eternal (see 1 Tim. 1:17).

- He is unchangeable (see Mal. 3:6).

- He is omnipotent, omniscient, and omnipresent (see Ps. 139:7-12; Isa. 46:10; Rom. 1:20).

- He is the Father of glory, the Father of lights, the Father of spirits, the Father of mercies, and He is the Father of our Lord Jesus Christ (see Rom. 1:7; 2 Cor. 1:3; Eph. 1:17; Heb. 12:9; James 1:17).

- He is light, and in Him is no darkness at all (see 1 John 1:5).

- He dwells in unapproachable light (see 1 Tim. 6:16).

- He wraps Himself with light (see Ps. 104:2).

- He shines in glory and splendor (see Rev. 21:23).

- He is not passive but is burning jealousy. He is a consuming fire (see Deut. 4:24).

- He is the Ancient of Days, and His very throne is on fire with wheels of fire, and it has a river of fire streaming from it (see Dan. 7:9).

- He is the Father in the parable of the lost son, and when the prodigal son was still a great way off, the Father saw His son, felt compassion for His son, ran to His son, fell on His son's neck, and kissed His son (see Luke 15:20).

- He is the Father who openly declares His affection over His sons and daughters (see 2 Pet. 1:17).

- He is a joyful Father, a righteous Father, a holy Father, a good Father, a just Father, and a kind Father (see Deut. 32:4; Luke 12:32; John 17:11, 25; Eph. 2:6).

- He is a merciful and compassionate Father (see Luke 6:36).

- He is a patient Father (see Rom. 15:5).

Jesus wanted us to know, when we pray, we are praying to our Father, and we must know who He is. We were made to worship Him—to gaze upon Him. He wants to remove the scales from our eyes so that we may see Him in all His glorious splendor. What better way to do this than in prayer! In prayer, we can encounter Him in all His multifaceted greatness.

ENCOUNTERING THE PLACE

When Jesus said, *"Our Father in heaven,"* He was connecting us to where our Father lives. He lifts our gaze to the throne room in Heaven. Not only does He want us to see the Father and recognize who He is, but Jesus wants us to see the significance of the place wherein the Father dwells. Jesus wants us to see the Father on the throne that is above every other throne. Jesus beckons us to Heaven that isn't only waiting for us after we die but is accessible now through faith in Him.

We have to know Heaven is real. It's where God lives. Jesus is in Heaven, sitting at God's right hand. Heaven is where God rules, where He sits enthroned. It's the place of dominion, authority, and preeminence over every power, principality, and dominion. And this is where prayer is birthed.

We are commanded in Scripture, *"If then you were raised with Christ, seek those things which are above, where Christ is, sitting at the right hand of God. Set your mind on things above, not on things on the earth"* (Col. 3:1-2).

We are told, *"Do not look at the things which are seen, but at the things which are not seen. For the things which are seen are temporary, but the things which are not seen are eternal"* (2 Cor. 4:18).

Scripture tells us to look up to where God is in Heaven. And Jesus told us to pray, *"Our Father in heaven."*

So, what's Heaven like? Who is there? What goes on there?

I don't necessarily have a proof text for what I'm about to say, but I believe Jesus was seeing what the apostle John described in Revelation 4. In other words, when Jesus was teaching the disciples to pray, His very thoughts were *"set on those things which are above."* He was looking *"at the things which are not seen"* here on the earth. He saw what John saw. And what John saw was an open door in Heaven, and then John heard a voice invite him to come up there. Next, we read:

Immediately I was in the Spirit; and behold, a throne set in heaven, and One sat on the throne. And He who sat there was like a jasper and a sardius stone in appearance; and there was a rainbow around the throne, in appearance like an emerald. Around the throne were twenty-four thrones, and on the thrones I saw twenty-four elders sitting, clothed in white robes; and they had crowns of gold on their heads. And from the throne proceeded lightnings, thunderings, and voices. Seven lamps of fire were burning before the throne, which are the seven Spirits of God. Before the throne there was a sea of glass, like crystal. And in the midst of the throne, and around the throne, were four living creatures full of eyes in front and in back. The first living creature was like a lion, the second living creature like a calf, the third living creature had a face like a man, and the fourth living creature was like a flying eagle. The four living creatures, each having six wings, were full of eyes around and within. And they do not rest day or night saying, "Holy, holy,

holy, Lord God Almighty, who was and is and is to come!" Whenever the living creatures give glory and honor and thanks to Him who sits on the throne, who lives forever and ever, the twenty-four elders fall down before Him who sits on the throne and worship Him who lives forever and ever, and cast their crowns before the throne, saying: "You are worthy, O Lord, to receive glory and honor and power; for You created all things, and by Your will they exist and were created" (Revelation 4:2-11).

This chapter is absolutely essential to your growing in your life of prayer. The first time I heard someone preach out of this chapter, I didn't understand a word of it, yet my spirit was deeply provoked. Afterward, I began to long for a greater intimacy with God. I wanted to see what John saw and to understand what it all meant.

John was doing his best to describe what he was seeing and was using words that were common to his day, but I'm sure those words didn't even touch the reality of what he was seeing. That's why he used the word *like*. The One who sat on the throne was *"like a jasper and a sardius stone,"* and the rainbow was *"like an emerald."*

We have a problem today, and that is we think we know enough about God and Heaven. We think our perceptions are accurate, but the truth is we see veiled through our religious lenses and skewed paradigms. King David said, *"Enlighten my eyes, lest I sleep the sleep of death,"* and *"Open my eyes, that I may see wondrous things from Your law"* (Ps. 13:3; 119:18). The apostle Paul prayed *"that the God of our Lord Jesus Christ, the Father of glory, may give to you the spirit of wisdom and revelation in the knowledge of Him, the eyes of your understanding being enlightened"* (Eph. 1:17-18). Like Jesus told the Laodicean church, we need to anoint our eyes with eye salve so we can see (see Rev. 3:18). We need to buy eye salve.

How do we buy eye salve?

We say, "Jesus, I need it! I need eye salve!" Our saying it is the currency we need to buy it.

Every phrase, however, of Revelation 4 is important to giving us a right perspective in prayer.

Why?

Because everything flows out of what we see or how we perceive God and where He lives. That being said, let's look more closely at several of the phrases in Revelation 4:

- *"And behold, a door standing open in heaven"* (v. 1). The foundation to prayer is the exhale that a door has been opened for us into Heaven. It is a welcome sign for us.

- *"Come up here, and I shall show you things"* (v. 1). Here is our official invitation to come and see things that God wants to reveal to us.

- *"A throne set in heaven"* (v. 2). When you pray, you're not simply talking to your Friend. You are approaching a throne set far above every throne, power, and dominion. Almighty God is enthroned over the nations, over the galaxies, and He is Your Father. His throne is set and is immovable.

- *"One sat on the throne"* (v. 2). Abba is on the throne. He is seated. *"Hear, O Israel: The Lord our God, the Lord is one!"* (Deut. 6:4). There is One greater than all, enthroned above all.

- *"Like a jasper"* (v. 3). In John's best attempt, he likens the One he is seeing to brilliant, blinding light—like jasper. John is seeing the many facets of the diamond that is the beauty of the Father.

- *"A sardius stone in appearance"* (v. 3). Not only is the Father light, but He is fiery like a ruby or sardius. Our God is a consuming fire. He isn't passive, distant, disconnected, indifferent, or aloof. He's engaged deeply and deliberately. He is a burning fire that is coming back again!

- *"A rainbow around the throne"* (v. 3). Mercy is over all His works, and it's in and through mercy that God relates to His creation. The rainbow is God's sign of mercy to us, and when He looks on it, He remembers *"the everlasting covenant"* between Him *"and every living creature of all flesh that is on the earth"* (Gen. 9:16). If it were not for His mercy, we would all be dead.

- *"Twenty-four elders sitting"* (v. 4). The greatest display of His mercy is the fact that He takes His former enemies—us—and through Christ gives us His righteousness, His throne, and His rewards. He takes enemies and makes them His ruling class.

- *"Clothed in white robes"* (v. 4). It's the real group of elders around the throne, and they are wearing white robes. Nothing speaks to what we have received in Christ like the words describing these elders. They are robed in righteousness, reminding us that He who didn't sin became sin so that we would *"become the righteousness of God in"* Christ (2 Cor. 5:21). I want you to know that, if you are in Christ, you are as clean as Jesus is clean, and you are as close as Jesus is close to God the Father because you're in Him and He's in you!

- *"Crowns of gold on their heads"* (v. 4). The crowns of the elders in Heaven represent realms of authority that God gives us through His grace. He crowns us with His glory and mercy, and He lets us participate in ruling and reigning with Him.

- *"From the throne proceeded lightnings, thunderings, and voices"* (v. 5). The lightning, thundering, and voices in Heaven remind us of what happens when the Church wakes up to who we are in Christ. It releases the prophetic spirit in power, glory, and creativity. I believe the Psalm 29 thunders are coming back to the pulpits. That's bringing Heaven to Earth when God thunders in His glory and power and majesty.

- *"Seven lamps of fire . . . the seven Spirits of God"* (v. 5). Then there are the seven Spirits of God burning before the throne. They are seven distinct operations of the Holy Spirit—the Spirit of the Lord, the Spirit of Wisdom, the Spirit of Understanding, the Spirit of Counsel, the Spirit of Knowledge, the Spirit of Might, and the Spirit of the Fear of the Lord (see Isa. 11:2).

- *"A sea of glass, like crystal"* (v. 6). The sea of glass is where we stand. This sea of glass is mingled with fire, and it's a translucent blue pavement where the knowledge of God is imparted.

- *"Four living creatures full of eyes in front and in back"* (v. 6). Try to picture them as John saw them. These were creatures filled with eyes. One creature was like a lion, one like an eagle, one like a calf, and one having a face of a man. These creatures are the burning ones who *"do not rest day or night, saying 'Holy, holy,*

holy'" (v. 8). These creatures have been in the same room with the same Person, singing the same word forever. They aren't only saying, "Pure, pure, pure," but are saying, "Totally other than, totally other than, totally other than." That's what holy means. It's like they're saying, "I've never seen Him like this before," and the crazy thing is they haven't. God is forever blowing their minds with fresh discoveries of His beauty, and they never get used to Him!

Jesus, in His first line of the Lord's prayer, takes us to Revelation 4 to set the eyes of our minds and hearts on where prayer begins: the throne room. Friend, when you pray, Jesus wants you to have a picture of Heaven and the activities going on around and about the throne. He wants you to know you have an open invitation to come up and worship and pray from your seat *"in the heavenly places in Christ Jesus"* (Eph. 2:6).

DECLARING HIS HOLINESS

Jesus told the disciples to pray to their Father in Heaven, *"Hallowed be Your name."* The one word that surrounds the throne is *holy.*

In our beginning in prayer, we must learn to ascend to the place where the Father is sitting on His throne. It's the shining, burning, emerald rainbow surrounding, twenty-four thrones encircling, lightnings and thunderings sounding, sea of glass encompassing, and eye bedazzled creatures declaring throne! Can you see it?

I find it hard to get past the fact that the creatures, who have been in the same room with the same Person, sing the same word forever. I get bored when we sing a worship song more than a couple of times. These creatures haven't even scratched the surface of seeing and knowing all of God, so every time their eyes lock onto something about the Father, they can't help but say, "Holy! Holy! Holy!"

Faith in prayer flows out of revelation—revelation of who God is and where He lives. And since revelation never stops, as we see in the worshipful response of the four creatures, faith continually flows out with fresh proclamations. In essence, Jesus taught His disciples and us to join in with the four living creatures full of eyes in declaring the Father's holiness—"Our Father in heaven, holy!"

DECREEING HIS KINGDOM AND WILL

"Your kingdom come. Your will be done on earth as it is in heaven" was what Jesus told them to decree. Note that prayer comes down from the place of revelation. Revelation accesses Heaven, and faith pulls it down.

As we become increasingly conscious of our heavenly home around the throne, and we learn to ascend into that realm, a prayer will come out of us. It will say, "Release this in our lives, in our families, in our marriages, in our finances, in our souls, in our churches, in our cities, and in the nations!"

From Heaven flows every prayer summed up in, *"Your kingdom come. Your will be done on earth as it is in heaven."* You can only release into your sphere of life what you are touching in Heaven. We must first ascend to the throne so that we may bring down the resources of Heaven.

Everything we need comes from our Father in Heaven, and so in the rest of the Lord's Prayer, Jesus addressed our daily needs, our receiving forgiveness and giving forgiveness, and our deliverance from temptation.

THE PARABLE

Without skipping a beat in Luke 11, Jesus then went into a second lesson on prayer by sharing a parable with the disciples. We need to see that, through this parable, Jesus was still answering the disciples' request to be taught to pray.

If the Lord's Prayer is Jesus teaching us how to walk through the open door into Heaven and to freely access what has been made available to us, this parable is how to persevere into seeing closed doors open in our lives, our families, and our circumstances. Put simply: Prayer is about walking through opened doors and opening closed doors.

So, after providing the disciples with a great paradigm for prayer, Jesus looked at them and basically said, "OK. You want to learn about prayer? Well, picture yourself asleep one night, and around midnight, you hear a loud, alarming knock at the door of your house.

"You're startled, right? You're awakened, and a thousand thoughts flood your mind of who could be at your door at this time of night. As you open the door, you're surprised to see your friend standing before you. He's been on a journey, so he's hungry and asks you for bread.

"You love this friend and desperately want to help him out, but a painful revelation hits you: You don't have any bread. You don't have any, yet you have a friend whom you know has bread and will give it to you. So, it's midnight, and you and your friend go to your other friend's house and begin to knock at his door, expecting an immediate response. But you hear a voice from the other side of the door, saying, 'Leave me alone. My children are with me in bed. It's late. Go away.'"

This story or analogy Jesus shared tells you there will come "midnight knocks" to the door of your life that will awaken you from your sleep, expose your inability to solve the problem in your own wisdom and resources, and drive you to your knees. Furthermore, His parable shows us that, in the midnight moment when we need God urgently, He doesn't move on our timetable. In fact, His slowness to act will feel as if He's resisting us.

What do you do then?

According to the parable, you keep praying, knowing who God is, what He possesses, and who you are to Him.

This is so important because, if you continue in your prayer life long enough, then you inevitably hit this wall where God is not breaking in according to your timetable. And you need to know what to do when that happens: You persevere.

It seems to me that there aren't many leaders who have persevered through this kind of long night and gone through to the other side. We need leaders who know how to keep knocking, keep asking, keep pursuing until God comes through with the bread!

I believe this moment where God is seemingly resisting us is the place where leaders are made. Leaders are the ones who don't quit and who press on and press into the release of fullness. Jesus said, *"Though he will not rise and give to him because he is his friend, yet because of his persistence he will rise and give to him as many as he needs"* (Luke 11:8).

What provoked the man inside his home to open the door at midnight? Was it friendship?

Not according to Jesus. The friend with the bread got up and gave the friend standing outside his house all that the friend outside needed because of the outside friend's persistence, not because of their friendship.

Jesus, then looked at His disciples and said,

> *So I say to you, ask, and it will be given to you; seek, and you will find; knock, and it will be opened to you. For everyone who asks receives, and he who seeks finds, and to him who knocks it will be opened. If a son asks for bread from any father among you, will he give him a stone? Or if he asks for a fish, will he give him a serpent instead of a fish? Or if he asks for an egg, will he offer him a scorpion? If you then, being evil, know how to give good gifts to your children, how much more will your heavenly Father give the Holy Spirit to those who ask Him!*
> (Luke 11:9-13)

It's sad to say this, but many times, it takes circumstantial crises to incite us to pray. God will throw us in the deep end of the pool, as it were, causing us to flail and kick and call out to Him. It's a rude awakening, for sure, that drives us to our knees. Prayer begins where we end.

Have you ever encountered a circumstance that you didn't see coming, and when it came, you found that you weren't strong enough or smart enough to get yourself out of it? Then, to top it all off, God wasn't breaking in when you needed Him to?

This, my friend, is where prayer begins and where prayer goes from a nice religious exercise to your heart frantically becoming fully engaged in petition. This is where leaders are formed into the image of Christ and where victories are won. The ones who don't quit but stay in the furnace are the ones who see God do wonders.

What keeps you in the furnace when everything around you says, "Quit!"?

The continual daily receiving and confession of who God is, what He possesses, His generous heart to give, and who you are to Him—these will keep you in the furnace.

The revelation of our good Father who will not give us something different than we are asking to "teach us a lesson" or hold out on us will keep us in the furnace.

Our God is a good Father who loves to give the Holy Spirit to those who ask Him. Remember He said, *"If you then, being evil, know how to give good gifts to your children, how much more will your heavenly Father give the Holy Spirit to those who ask Him!"* (Luke 11:13).

Let me say this another way. I want to speak to you in today's language: You do not have a jacked up, twisted Father in Heaven who answers your prayers by creating harm or difficulty. He doesn't respond to your sincere request by giving you things to hurt you. *No!* He is a good, kind, generous Father who gives you the very thing you're asking for. If we, having twisted intentions, have the capacity for generosity, *how much more* will our heavenly Father give the Holy Spirit to those who ask Him.

This is the climax of Jesus' teaching on prayer. He is good, and no matter what walls you hit, don't quit. Just keep coming and asking because He's good, He loves you, and He will answer you.

In twenty years of doing daily prayer meetings, I've found countless people hit this wall. Afterward, I've seen them slowly and subtly begin to withdraw their hearts from God and settle for a safe form of Christianity. They couldn't handle what they thought was going to end in disappointment. Don't do like I've seen so many others do. Don't back off. Lean in and ask our Father again.

It's in the furnace where all of the wrong views of God are brought to the surface.

It's in the furnace where we cast down arguments and lies that exalt themselves against the knowledge of God.

It's in the furnace where we declare the truth of who our Father is over and over and over again.

It's in the furnace where we declare who we are to Him over and over and over again.

It's in the furnace where we wait and just burn before Him.

The furnace is where the new breed continues to be fashioned and shaped. It's where we are forged in the fire of delayed promises. We are delivered from fantasies of grandeur and are conformed into the image of the Son.

The new breed of followers and leaders are the ones who stay—the ones who don't quit! We know what God has promised He is able to fulfill. We pioneer into the bakery of Heaven and become distributors of the life of Christ to a lost world, giving them as much as the world needs.

I believe there are midnight wrestles with God that change us forever. We may have a limp forever, but we also walk with an open Heaven over our lives as God gives us divine resource whenever we need it.

So, when you pray, pray!

CULTIVATING THE SPIRIT OF PRAYER

4

"HOUSE OF WISDOM"

"IF YOU BUILD IT, I WILL COME." THAT'S WHAT I HEARD THE
Holy Spirit speak to me a few years ago. In that moment,
I became acutely aware that God wants to release His fullness. He wants vessels of the Lord to carry His presence and
power. And if you and I build these containers, He will fill
them. He will come.

One of my greatest burdens for you as you read this and
for this generation as a whole is to understand that the spirit
of prayer falls on the life of prayer.

What do I mean by this?

My definition for the spirit of prayer is the deep awareness and confidence that I have God's ear, God's heart, and
God's hand. There is nothing greater in the whole world
than walking in unity with God, communing with Him, and
releasing His will into the earth, but this confidence is developed in a certain place: in the life of prayer. The life of prayer
is the practical, mundane choices that we make every day to

prioritize a time and a place, and never let anything or anyone get in the way of this holy place between us and God.

So many of us live off of impartations at conferences, YouTube worship songs, and streamed services, yet many of us have never been able to build a consistent life of prayer. Whether it be distraction, shame, or busyness, we never seem to continue in consistency in our prayer lives, and we slowly find ourselves running on empty and in need of another touch. I totally get this and have done it myself, but there has to be a point where we get tired of the cycle and long for something deeper and more fulfilling in our lives.

Building a time and place for God to come and fill is one of the strongest prophetic words that I believe the Holy Spirit is speaking to the Church in this hour. This isn't sexy, but it's the ancient paths that God said would restore us to a rest that we've been longing for.

I'm convinced that the cultivation of our prayer lives has more to do with how we spend our time, our money, and our energy than we could ever realize.

The greatest battleground in our day is where the forces of distraction fight against the cultivation of the life and spirit of prayer. As a parent of two teenage daughters, I'm fully aware of the constant bombardment of voices, images, and videos that are screaming for their attention. Whether it be through the phone, television, or iPad, we are under a siege from the enemy to steal our time.

The statistics of video game use is absolutely staggering. Sixty percent of Americans play video games daily, more than

2.5 billion people are gamers in the world, and that gaming is a 148.8 billion-dollar industry![4]

The statistics say 90.4 percent of Millennials, 77.5 percent of Gen Xers, and 48.2 percent of Baby Boomers are active social media users, and people spend on average 3 hours per day on social media and messaging.[5] And I'm not even including statistics on television viewing, livestream watching, pornography use, or cellphone or device usage.

Additionally, many in our day and age are suffering from extended adolescence, where they never enter adulthood through the rites of passage and are stuck in this middle place of no vision. Many twenty-somethings today, for example, are still living at home or are still living financially dependent on their parents. Just listen to your friends and neighbors around you talk about their young adult children returning to what was once their "empty nest." One group of adolescent health experts has even argued that we should stretch the adolescence phase from the current 10–19 years of age to 10–24 years of age.[6]

Though it pains me concerning the obstacles and the reality of the generations today, I'm filled with great faith and confidence in God's ability to bring us all into the fullness of our destinies. But it's going to require something of us.

God is going to take the most distracted and addicted generation and call us to a place of divine encounter with Him. I believe with all my heart that God will win the beauty contest at the end of the age and will awaken a bored generation to the revelation of Jesus Christ.

REHAB

When Jesus taught us to pray, He told us, *"Go into your room, and when you have shut your door, pray to your Father who is in the secret place"* (Matt. 6:6).

This shutting of the door is intentionally cutting off all the media outlets and making a time and place with God sacred. We meet with Him on a daily basis in the secret place. This will take a deliberate setting of our wills. As we begin in our journey, it will feel as if we entered a rehab center as we begin to detox from all the messages, comments, likes, and emojis that have kept us glued to our screens for much longer than they should have.

We must swim against the currents of the culture and ask God to deliver us from the cancer of the human heart called boredom with God.

He has been stunning seraphim throughout the ages. They have yet to exhaust all of His glory! They've never gotten used to Him, and they never will, and you never will.

We're so small in our capacities and so limited in our depth of experience in true joy and entertainment because we have stuffed ourselves with all this other false entertainment and fleeting pleasure. This has resulted in our having no appetite for the best things or, more specifically, for the one thing.

I believe that one of the most besetting sins in this generation is laziness.

The wisest man ever, Solomon, wrote the book of Proverbs, and in this book, he wrote a great deal on laziness and how much damage it can do to the spiritual as well as the overall life of a believer:

> *The soul of a lazy man desires, and has nothing; but the soul of the diligent shall be made rich* (13:4).
> *Laziness casts one into a deep sleep, and an idle person will suffer hunger* (19:15).
> *The lazy man will not plow because of winter; he will beg during harvest and have nothing* (20:4).
> *Much food is in the fallow ground of the poor* (13:23).

There is much food in the unbroken ground of our souls because we never cultivated our interior lives. We were called to cultivate our gardens, and yet because of laziness, we never discover what is truly inside us. The lazy person will make excuses, state they haven't been given what they need, and yet the whole time it was right there before them. We must cultivate our interior lives as well as put to work the gifts God has given us, for *"he who tills his land will be satisfied with bread"* (Prov. 12:11).

It's time to detox from our addiction to the blue light and the other things that have gotten all up and on us from the culture around us. We need to sweat out the saturation of the culture and this age. We need to place ourselves into a concentrated environment of prayer and fasting and giving.

I believe that the call to early morning prayer especially releases the death blow to the spirit of laziness found in our sleeping habits. Solomon connected laziness and sleep together in a profound way. He wrote, *"Do not love sleep, lest you come to poverty; open your eyes, and you will be satisfied with bread"* (Prov. 20:13).

In Luke 22:45, Jesus found His disciples *"sleeping from sorrow,"* which means they were not accustomed to navigating dark nights of heaviness. He had told them moments before to watch and pray lest they entered into temptation (see Luke 22:40). But, under the weight of the hour, they had been unable to stay awake and pray. Later on, after His arrest, all succumbed to the temptation to leave the Lord.

I believe waking up early in the morning and declaring war on our beds are practical ways to declare war on heaviness and slumber. Not only can this prepare us to fight temptation, but it also can be used to broaden and deepen our capacities for more of Him.

WISDOM

We must understand that God first establishes a structure, a container, to house the reality that He will fill it with. Proverbs 24:3-4 affirms, *"Through wisdom a house is built, and by understanding it is established; by knowledge the rooms are filled with all precious and pleasant riches."*

It's the life of wisdom that can be filled with the Spirit of Revelation. In fact, the house of wisdom houses the Spirit of Revelation.

I believe revelation sees the end, and wisdom walks out the journey to get there. Another way to say this is revelation fuels the life of wisdom, and wisdom makes revelation a reality. So, we need both wisdom and revelation.

I like to explain the importance of these two things in this way. When we fly somewhere, for example, we need to know where we're flying before we ever get on a plane, and we can't get to where we're going if we don't get on the right plane.

Let's say that I receive a revelation, and the revelation is a trip to Singapore. The trip to Singapore provides me with the vision of going to Singapore. This requires me to take some steps to get to my revealed destination. I book a flight that flies out of the nearest airport that connects to another flight that will take me to Singapore. I can't just choose any flight. I have to choose the particular flight that will take me to the hub city at which I will disembark that plane and walk to a different gate to board the final flight that will take me to Singapore. I can't just randomly pick a gate and a plane. No, I must pick *the* planes and *the* gates that will get me to Singapore.

That is wisdom. It's the practical daily steps I take to get to my destination. Revelation in our spiritual lives is the excellency of the knowledge of Christ Jesus our Lord. He, then, is our ultimate destination.

We want to grow in the Spirit of Revelation, and revelation fills the house of wisdom. Remember that wisdom builds the house; therefore, we must seek to build a life of daily practical choices that position us to receive revelation.

The Spirit of Revelation falls upon the life of prayer, and the life of prayer doesn't happen by accident. The life of prayer has chosen an intentional, consistent time and place to meet with God.

I'm not saying we can earn the Spirit of Revelation. What I am saying is we can honor it by building a life that is conducive to the preciousness of what we are receiving. With raising kids, there are levels of maturity that qualify my children for greater responsibilities. I don't give my car keys to my seven-year-old because she has no appreciation for what I'm giving her, neither does she have the maturity to put the keys to use and drive my car.

We must understand there is a structure that God is looking for. It's built by wisdom. It's built by our making those daily decisions to increase our capacities. And He will fill our houses because concrete action toward God gets Heaven's attention.

THE FOUNDATION

Before we even can get to the practical aspects of wisdom, we must even go to a deeper foundation on which wisdom rests: It's the fear of the Lord. We are told in Proverbs 9:10, *"The fear of the Lord is the beginning of wisdom."*

What is the fear of the Lord?

In a general sense, the fear of the Lord is the awareness of God. It's the living awareness that He is, He sees, He hears, He cares, and He responds accordingly.

The fear of the Lord causes us to live the same when we are around many people as when we are alone. It makes the prayer room and the bedroom the same for us because we understand that there is no place hidden from the gaze of God. The fear of the Lord knows that what we do in secret is as important as what we do in public.

The fear of the Lord removes hypocrisy as it brings with it the deep conviction that everything matters. There is no waste of time, energy, finance, or resource. Everything is sacred. Everything is noticed by God, moves God, and provokes a response from Him. Cups of cold water, acts of forgiveness, prayers of blessing—these all move God more than we can even imagine.

I believe one of the first emotions we will feel once we cross over to the other side of eternity is amazement that He ever paid such attention to *everything*. I can imagine thinking, *I can't believe that I, Corey Russell, could have such a deep impact on You, my Eternal Father.*

The Spirit of Wisdom is living a life in the fear of the Lord and understanding God is scanning the earth, looking for lives of wisdom and lives of dependence that He can release His glory in and through.

WHERE IS HIS HOUSE?

The God who sits in Heaven and rests His feet on the earth— the God who has made everything and is surrounded by millions of angels incessantly declaring who He is—said this:

> *"Heaven is My throne, and earth is My footstool. Where is the house that you will build Me? And*

where is the place of My rest? For all those things My hand has made, and all those things exist," says the Lord. "But on this one will I look: on him who is poor and of a contrite spirit, and who trembles at My word" (Isaiah 66:1-2).

Our God looks at you and me today and asks one question: "Where is the house that you will build Me?"

There is one thing in all the universe that God either won't make or can't make, and that's your voluntary decision and agreement with His leadership in your life to build Him a resting place. You much choose to build the container.

"On this one will I look"—there is a heart, a life that gets the attention of Heaven. It's the poor spirit, the leaning spirit, the responsive spirit.

There is a life that catches the attention of God. It's a life that isn't confident in itself but is broken, tender, and responsive to His Word.

The word *contrite* means lame and broken, so God is actually looking for the broken, dependent, interior life in which to make His home. There is a depth of brokenness that God works in the soul of man that prepares him for God's glory.

God sits in Heaven and puts His feet on the earth, and He looks to you and me and asks, *"Where is the house that you will build for Me?"*

There is a house that only you can build for Him. I can't build it for you. You can't build it for me. This is the container, the house, or the wineskin that He will fill with His glory.

When God finds a person, who is responsive to His Word—someone who trembles at His Word—He quickly breaks in to make His home in that person.

In Jesus' first public message, what we call *the Sermon on the Mount*, Jesus told us that poverty of spirit is the secret to the blessed life (Matt. 5:3). He also said that the one who hears and responds to His message will be like a wise man who built his house on the rock:

> *Therefore whoever hears these sayings of Mine, and does them, I will liken him to a wise man who built his house on the rock: and the rain descended, the floods came, and the winds blew and beat on that house; and it did not fall, for it was founded on the rock* (Matthew 7:24-25).

God is calling us to be wise builders. So, in the fear of the Lord, we will awaken early from our sleep and declare what the psalmist David did, *"O God, You are my God; early will I seek You; my soul thirsts for You; my flesh longs for You in a dry and thirsty land where there is no water"* (Ps. 63:1). That cry, that expression of longing, coupled with your rising early will get God's attention. Then go to your prayer closet. Shut the door. Meet your Father first thing in the morning at a consistent place and time, praise Him, worship Him, open His Word, meditate upon it, pray, and wait upon Him.

Build a house for Him, and He will come!

5

BUILDING A LIFE OF PRAYER

IN 2003, GOD VISITED ME IN A POWERFUL WAY AND gave me what I believe to be the vision and values that we need to embrace to become the new breed of believers, leaders, and missionaries. The vision is for us to lead and preach from the mount of divine vision, but we first need to ascend this holy mountain. That's where the values come in. The values are important in enabling us to make that ascent.

A DIVINE ENCOUNTER

I remember the day back in 2003 when God visited me. I was sitting in a meeting with about twenty other pastors from our community, listening intently to the speaker sharing, when one of the pastors who was sitting behind me began to whisper to me about a dream his wife had had the night before. The pastor behind me got my attention as he explained that, in his wife's dream, she saw a huge hardcover Old English book entitled *The History of Revival*. As she opened the pages, she began to read of different revivalists in history and the accounts of what happened in their respective revivals. She read chapters from John Wesley, George Whitefield, Jonathan Edwards, Charles Finney, and others, and then she came to a chapter with my name on it as the chapter title! She had gone in the future and had begun to read of the accounts of revival associated with me, my ministry, and my generation.

As the pastor shared this latter part with me, I experienced something that I had never experienced before and haven't experienced again to this day. I began to feel a wind come around me and surround me like I imagine a whirlwind would do. Before I knew it, I was in the middle of a divine encounter.

For two hours, as this wind whipped around me, I kept hearing the same two statements over and over again. The first one was, "Corey, you haven't seen the grace that I'm about to release on a generation for prayer, fasting, and consecration." And the second one was, "But it's got to be done together with brothers and sisters in community."

As I heard these statements, I was struck by the confidence in God's voice. It told me that there was a grace, a supernatural ability, to pray, fast, and live set apart like nothing the world had ever seen before. It was like God had an ace up His sleeve, and He was about to drop that card on the planet. Suddenly, there would be men and women of prayer, fasting, and holiness like at no other time in history!

Immediately after this encounter, I knew the Lord was calling me to start "holy clubs" with young men and women, having them begin to pray, fast, and grow closer together in community. The term *Holy Club* was actually a derogatory term that students in Oxford University used toward a group started in 1729 by John and Charles Wesley. The group also included George Whitefield. "The club members set aside time for praying, examining their spiritual lives, studying the Bible, and meeting together. In addition, they took food to poor families, visited lonely people in prison, and taught orphans how to read."[7] They did this as they spent several evenings together each week. The group provided a method of discipleship and community that tutored the Wesleys and Whitefield into becoming the great awakeners that they were.

Soon, I called three young men and a couple of young women, and we decided that we would wake up at four o'clock and do early morning prayer from half past four until half past five before we came into the prayer room and did a six to noon watch Tuesday through Thursday. We also decided we would fast Tuesdays and Wednesdays. We would gather at my house and then go do prophetic evangelism on Tuesday evenings while we would wait on the Lord together at my house on Thursday evenings. We ended up doing this for about six months and had many powerful times together in the Holy Spirit. The testimonies of divine encounter and fruitfulness were staggering.

In the middle of all of this, however, I began to see an elite spirit rise up in the young people, and it had a religious bent to it. I began to hear them make statements like, "They're really not *praying* in the prayer room," or "No one is going after God like us." This kept increasing until I began to see that, if I didn't shut it down, we would be in trouble. I went ahead and shut it down, and I was really frustrated because I knew the encounter that I had received in 2003 was authentic. I knew God was calling me to something, and yet I was finding that my leadership was not producing the kind of fruit that I desired.

It wouldn't be for another four years, in 2008, before God would stir this vision back up and give me a place in which to express it. A door opened in our school for me to lead third-and fourth-year students in something we were calling, "The Apostolic Prayer and Preaching School." We had around thirty-five to fifty students who signed up voluntarily to take this program, which meant they truly desired to run with others in pressing in for all of what God wanted to do in and through them.

Since the group was quite large, I knew we would need to divide the one group into several others comprised of five to seven people. I put guys with guys and girls with girls. One of the values that we wanted to include with the prayer, fasting, and preaching was accountability around themes like pornography, self-hatred, etc. We wanted to create safe places to talk about secretive things such as these.

My desire was to create a context in which students could be assisted in developing in the life and spirit of prayer as well as in the revelation of the Word as they had expressed their desire. These young people were aspiring preachers and teachers of the Word, and these are holy callings. Convinced that we must aid them in the preparation of their souls and lives to steward the Word of God and bear up under the pressures that ministry would bring, we trained them in cultivating the following values:

- Early morning prayer
- Weekly and monthly fasting
- Praying in tongues for extended periods of time
- Meditation in the Bible
- Mercy-based accountability
- Sleep, recreation, and exercise
- Preaching

Through the years, I've seen the application of these values forever change the lives of those who have cultivated them. It's my sincere belief that, should you apply these to your life, they will transform you as well.

As I have walked through my own trials and tribulations through the years, a profound tenderness, patience, gentleness, and understanding of the grace and mercy of God with us in the process has marked me deeply.

There are no superheroes in the Kingdom. There are simply weak people who long for more and who don't give up. Every one of us are like distracted two-year-olds who can barely focus and make eye contact with God, yet the very weak reaching of our hearts moves Him and releases grace upon us to follow Him.

The values I'm about to walk you through are for everyone, not just elite, super-spiritual people, but weak people like you and me. We must bring our weakness before God and exchange it for His strength.

VALUE 1: EARLY MORNING PRAYER

The alarm goes off at 5:30 a.m. I quickly reach for my phone to turn it off. I lie there for a couple of seconds, tired, sleepy, asking myself, *Why am I up?* Then a thought hits me, *I've never ever regretted getting up early to be with Jesus.*

Early morning prayer has changed my life. I don't know how it happened or when it happened, but I discovered a glorious secret that has revolutionized my life: Make Jesus the first Person you look at, the first Person you hear, and the first Person you talk to, and it will shift the rest of your day.

One of the biggest keys in cultivating a consistent prayer life is building a consistent time and place to meet with the Lord every day and not missing that meeting for anything in the world. (I know I keep repeating this, but it's the best advice I can give anyone wanting to develop a life of prayer.) This will work in any time period, but I'm convinced that early morning prayer is the most helpful to establishing a prayer lifestyle.

I want to highlight the things that I've found to be true by committing to early morning prayer.

1. My prayer life has been formed in early morning prayer.

It's here that I learned to become a receiver and a listener. In Isaiah 50:4, the Lord said, *"He awakens Me morning by morning, He awakens My ear to hear as the learned."*

It's in early morning prayer that I learned to "be" instead of "do."

It's here that I learned to inhale and exhale His presence and His Word.

It's here that I learned the power of slowly and quietly whispering the Bible back to Jesus and entering into dialogue with Him.

It's here that I learned how to slowly and quietly commune with the Holy Spirit.

Over the past twenty years, I've found that, when my mind is the quietest, I pray the best. That's probably why Jesus prayed in the morning: *"Now in the morning, having risen a long while before daylight, He went out and departed to a solitary place; and there He prayed"* (Mark 1:35).

2. Early morning prayer saved me from stupid decisions after 10:00 p.m. because I've made many stupid decisions after 10:00 p.m.

I've found that most of the dumbest and shameful decisions I've made happened after 10 p.m. It was when I was tired with my guard down and I was surfing on the TV, computer, or phone that some image came up and I looked a little too long.

There have been other times when I've stayed up too late talking with someone, and many times the conversations ventured into talking about someone else. With both of our guards down, we spoke way too flippantly about that person, and then I personally felt the Spirit grieved by the things I said and other things I agreed with about that person.

I've known the pain of waking up after these nights and feeling that cloud of shame just resting on me as I've said, "I cannot believe that I did that, saw that, said that, or listened and agreed with that." The time when I could be drinking in the sweetness of Jesus' love was then filled with the traffic in my soul as I swam upstream against my shame and guilt, clinging to His blood and forgiveness. He always forgives. He always shows compassion and mercy when I come to Him, and yet I'm always freshly pained over allowing anything to steal my connection and peace with Him.

As I've discipled young people through the years, most of their greatest sins, shames, and regrets happened after 10:00 p.m. It's in light of this that I've come up with a revelation ☺. Let's get to bed by 10:00 p.m. Then let's get up around 6:00 a.m. I would rather see you looking tired and looking for the bed rather than looking for that old girlfriend or old boyfriend on Facebook.

The traffic that I've seen removed in my own life and the lives of those who have built their prayer lives around the early morning is astounding. Our prayer lives have gone from the roller coaster ride of praying when we feel like it and not praying when we don't to praying consistently each day at a specific time and place. In this routine and schedule, the spirit of prayer begins to touch our lives, and intimacy, revelation, and authority come upon us.

I've been a part of a prayer ministry that has gone day and night for over twenty years, so I love every time of the day and believe in the importance of every time of the day as far as it relates to establishing a prayer life. Some people are night people. They feel they are at their best then, and I totally get that. Others pray better in the middle of their day. I love anytime because anytime is a good time to pray.

When it comes to developing a lifestyle of prayer, however, I do believe practicing early morning prayer for a season establishes the priority of prayer for the rest of your life. Setting a prayer time in the morning establishes self-government over other areas in your life.

3. Early morning prayer has increased the Spirit of Revelation on my life.

One of the greatest benefits I've found in my life in early morning prayer is the abundance of revelation that flows in that first hour with the Lord. It reminds me of how the Lord rained down manna every morning in the wilderness for the children of Israel. He required them to get it before the sun got too hot (see Exod. 16:21).

It's in those first minutes of the day with my mind quiet, my heart and Bible open, and my ear on His chest that His voice is so clear, so loud, and so impactful. It's in this time that verses of the Bible or lyrics from a song or divine thoughts and emotions begin to flood my soul.

When God's voice is the first voice you hear in the morning, it brings alignment to every other voice you hear throughout your day.

4. Early morning prayer recalibrates me to His lovingkindness.

I'm addicted to early morning prayer simply because it's in those first minutes before dawn that He tells me again of His love and tenderness toward me. The kisses of His Word touch my heart, washing away fear, shame, and guilt. As the Son rises, I see Him, myself, and others through the lens of love. The psalmist David understood this as he wrote, *"Cause me to hear Your lovingkindness in the morning"* (Ps. 143:8).

Fresh tears roll down my face as I hear and receive again what He thinks about me and says about me. I fall freshly in love with Him every morning, and it centers me in His love.

5. Early morning prayer is a sacrifice.

It was early in the morning when the Lord spoke to Abraham to take his son, Abraham's only son, to the mountains and sacrifice him (see Gen. 22).

Some of the hardest things I've heard from God came first thing in the morning. When I've been there soaking in His love and meditating in His Word, His tender yet firm voice breaks in as He confronts something in me, reminds me of a conversation that I had with someone, and requires that I make it right. There have been countless times when God spoke directly to me about people with whom I needed to go and make wrong things right, people to whom I needed to give, or areas in my life that I needed to fast or abstain from. It's in the early morning where God has given me instruction or direction for the day.

6. Early morning prayer is where I give my wife and daughters the gift of stored prayers before they awake.

One of the gifts that I want to give my wife and daughters every day is stored prayers for them. I want them to awake into prayers for the Spirit of Revelation, encounters in the love of God, protection, peace, joy, and righteousness in the Holy Spirit.

We want to meet God at the dawning of each day, communing and fellowshipping with Him. We ascend to the mount of vision from the place of early morning prayer.

VALUE 2: WEEKLY AND MONTHLY FASTING

If I were on my death bed, and you were to ask me what three things have brought about the greatest impact in my spiritual life, without hesitating I would say fasting, meditation, and praying in the Spirit. These three things combined have accelerated my life in God like nothing else.

Though I've been on longer fasts, the fasts that have influenced my life the most have been regular weekly and monthly fasts. The one to two days weekly and three days monthly have served as a "spiritual chiropractic" adjustment to my life in the Word and the Spirit.

I want to say clearly that fasting as well as all spiritual disciplines do not earn us anything from God. These are gifts from God to make us vulnerable to the truth of who we already are in Christ. Our minds need renewing so that we can approve the full will of God in our lives, and fasting weakens our internal resistance to it and to the truth of the Word of God.

When truth impacts us in fasting, it hits harder, goes deeper, and shifts us quicker into alignment with Heaven.

How Fasting Affects Your Life

Let's look at some of the ways fasting has affected my life over the past twenty years.

1. Fasting quiets my soul and causes my spirit to rise within me.

We live in such a noisy and chaotic culture. It's filled with nonstop voices, pictures, and allurements. All of these affect our interior lives far more than we realize.

I'll be honest. I spend way too much time on Instagram, Twitter, and Facebook. Looking, reading, watching friends and strangers sharing their lives, hearing their stories, viewing their families, and reading their controversial statements that provoke debates entertain me far more than they should. I need a constant shift in my interior life that delivers me from this addiction. And fasting does this.

Over one to two days of fasting, my busy mind, emotions, and desires begin to subside and move to the back seat, and I then sense my spirit man come to the front seat. Usually, it takes about half the first day for this to take place. But once it does, my spirit ascends, and though weak and many times foggy in my mind, I begin to become aware that I simply belong to God—*"Surely I have calmed and quieted my soul, like a weaned child with his mother; like a weaned child is my soul within me"* (Ps. 131:2).

It's in this place that I begin to hear His whispers. He speaks in the quiet of my soul of who I am to Him. He speaks to me in His Word. He speaks to me about my girls. He speaks to me about other people.

Sometimes, I don't hear anything, but in the place of fasting, I come out of what I do for God and come into the realization of who I am to God. The Abba cry of Romans 8:15 grows within me, and it's here that I experience quiet and rest from all the images, voices, and noises that have crept into my soul.

2. The Word grows louder and clearer in fasting.

In Deuteronomy 8, God identified the purpose of His having taken the children of Israel through the wilderness en route to the Promised Land:

> *And you shall remember that the Lord your God led you all the way these forty years in the wilderness, to humble you and test you, to know what was in your heart, whether you would keep His commandments or not. So He humbled you, allowed you to hunger, and fed you with manna which you did not know nor did your fathers know, that He might make*

you know that man shall not live by bread alone;
but man lives by every word that proceeds from the
mouth of the Lord (vv. 2-3).

In fasting, God allows that which is in our hearts to be exposed, and He begins to feed us on His Word.

As a preacher, I know about reading the Word, studying the Word, writing the Word, and spending a lot of time around the Word; however, it's in and through fasting that I begin to savor the Word. He kisses the depths of my spirit man with His Word, and it touches me in ways that effect change.

It's in fasting that the Word goes from a tapping hammer to a sledgehammer. Fasting silences all the other voices in my life until I only hear one voice: the voice of the Beloved. I get drawn into the text, feeling the text, seeing the text, and encountering the Man on the other side of the pages.

If you have difficulty focusing on God when you read the Bible or difficulty understanding what you read, I want to encourage you to start fasting and watch what happens over six months.

3. Fasting increases hunger.

That's deep revelation, isn't it ☺? But, seriously, fasting awakens the primal ache for Jesus alone. Mourning, aching, and longing emerge in your soul. Fasting delivers you from domestication in your spiritual life, making you raw and desperate for Jesus and His presence. Fasting brings you into contact with your need for God.

I can't tell you how many times over the last twenty years that fasting cut me deeply, releasing in me a hunger for more and more of Jesus, and yet filled me at the same time. As Jesus said in Matthew 5:6, *"Blessed are those who hunger and thirst for righteousness, for they shall be filled."*

4. Fasting delivers me from the fear of man.

Fasting sets me apart from you and your opinions about me. When you are free from someone, you can love them freely. Today, so many ministers live bound by the fear of man and what others will think or what will happen if they say controversial things, unpopular truths, or talk about difficult passages in the Bible. Fasting sets you free from that so you can say what God says.

At the same time, fasting tenderizes you to say the hard stuff in the right spirit. We've all heard the preacher say the right verse but preach it in the wrong spirit. Fasting brings grace and truth together in a beautiful way. There is a way to say hard things with a tender spirit, and I've found fasting to bring these two things together.

Fasting helps me to articulate what I want to say with greater clarity. There have been times when I have had to have a difficult personal conversation with someone, and fasting helps me say what I want to, in the right spirit, without beating around the bush, giving a hundred disclaimers, or avoiding having the conversation in the first place.

5. Fasting delivers me from a political spirit, a networking spirit, and selfish ambition.

We desperately need a new breed of leaders who are freed from these three things. Whatever energy you have expended to generate ministry opportunities, you will have to exert even more to keep or maintain them. This is what saps all spiritual life and vitality. Fasting, on the other hand, frees you from these toxic realities and settles you in the truth that a man can only receive that which has been given to him from Heaven. No amount of striving, exploitation, or manipulation will fulfill you.

Fasting exposes the futility of climbing the ministry ladder. You see it for what it is. It's simply selfish ambition and manipulation.

Biblical Benefits of Fasting

The Bible shows us the many benefits of fasting. Here are a few that have deeply strengthened me in my own life.

1. Fasting reinforces sonship—our belovedness to the Father, our authority in the Spirit, and our inheritance in Christ.

In Matthew 3, Jesus began His ministry by being baptized by John. Then the Father opened the heavens and publicly declared, *"This is My beloved Son, in whom I am well pleased"* (v. 17). Jesus received this from His Father and then immediately went into the wilderness of fasting and prayer (see Matt. 4:1-2).

It's in the wilderness of fasting and prayer that the revelation of Jesus' Sonship was solidified as the devil sought to tempt Him to operate outside of His identity as the Son. Twice the devil said to Jesus, *"If You are the Son of God,"* pressing Him to do things to prove His identity (Matt. 4:3, 5).

If you want to grow in your identity as a son or daughter of God, add fasting to your life. You must understand that this will stir up voices within and without that will tempt you to prove yourself but stay connected to the Father's voice over your life. His voice will remind you who He is to you and who you are to Him—His beloved child. From this place, you have an inheritance and the authority to declare, *"Away with you, Satan! For it is written. . ."* (Matt. 4:10). And the enemy will depart, and angels will come and minister to you (see Matt. 4:11).

2. Fasting expresses longing and desire for the return of the Bridegroom, which will one day culminate in His return.

In Matthew 9:14, John's disciples asked why they and the Pharisees fasted often, yet they didn't see Jesus' disciples doing the same. Jesus said to them, *"Can the friends of the bridegroom mourn as long as the bridegroom is with them?"* (Matt. 9:15). Then, later in verse 15, Jesus told them that a time would come when the Bridegroom would be taken away and *"then they [would] fast."*

In this passage, Jesus calls us all to fast, not out of obligation or religious duty, but out of longing. Fasting in the New

Testament is born out of a longing and desire for the presence of Jesus.

I believe this will prove to be the new wineskins that God will entrust apostolic government, resource, and impact to in the coming days. The leaders who fast, not out of an attempt to prove something, but to express longing for Him will be given leadership in the Church in the coming days.

Fasting increases mourning for Him.

Fasting releases revelation of Jesus as the Bridegroom.

3. Fasting brings breakthrough as it bolsters authority and power in the individual believer's life.

Matthew 17:14-21 tells us a story of an epileptic boy whom Jesus healed after the disciples were unable to minister healing to him.

Later on, in private, the disciples asked Jesus why it was they could not deliver the boy from the demon that was causing him to have seizures. Jesus said, *"This kind does not go out except by prayer and fasting"* (v. 21).

There are simply realms of breakthrough in your life and in the lives of others that will only come about when you add fasting to your prayer life. We must not only live this out as believers, but must also train others to add fasting to confront the seemingly insurmountable obstacles, difficulties, and trials in their lives.

4. Fasting together as a corporate body of believers brings greater accountability and grace.

The prophet Joel, in his second chapter, declared twice, *"Blow the trumpet in Zion"* (vv. 1, 15). The first trumpet blast was issued to awaken the people to what was coming if they continued to live in compromise. The second trumpet blast was meant to call the people to respond by gathering together in fasting and prayer.

I believe the call to us as the new breed of believers and messengers is to be trumpets in our spheres of influence. We issue the sound that gathers people together for solemn assemblies of prayer and fasting.

Fasting alone, of course, is powerful, but I've found in my life that, when I fast with others, I encounter greater accountability and grace. When we all press in together, we encourage each other to keep going.

The early Church was born out of a corporate prayer and fasting meeting. Corporate meetings released fresh outpourings in the early Church. We must return to this.

5. Accumulated prayer and fasting over time releases angelic activity and fresh revelation.

In the life of Daniel, we see this to be true. More specifically, in Daniel 9-10, Daniel went on extended fasts that released unprecedented revelation concerning both the past generations and the generation of the Messiah's return.

I believe God is going to cause prophetic messengers to arise in these days. They will receive revelation concerning the end times rooted in the Scriptures upon which they have been meditating. Angels will bring them insight and revelation as they fast through the years.

6. A lifestyle of fasting cultivates the forerunner spirit.

Speaking of John the Baptist, Jesus said that he fasted and didn't drink wine (Luke 7:33). John the Baptist was the forerunner before the First Coming of Jesus. He was a man given to prayer and fasting in the wilderness.

I believe those given to fasting and praying in the wilderness will be among the forerunners of the Second Coming of Jesus.

There are many more benefits that neither time nor space allow me to enumerate, but permit me to list several here in an effort to provoke you to further study:

- Fasting separates voices from echoes.
- Fasting purifies our voices.
- Fasting humbles the proud areas in our souls.
- Fasting causes the areas of shame, guilt, and fear to manifest so that they can be addressed.
- Fasting tenderizes the religious areas in us.
- Fasting corrects the crooked ways in us.

Practicing Fasting

Now that you've seen some of the benefits of fasting and what it has accomplished in my life, you may wonder how to begin. Well, to start, I would recommend fasting one day a week. Perhaps you could aim at getting through your day without eating and then breaking your fast at dinner time. I would be faithful with this one day to dinner for several months.

At the end of those months, I would seek to fast through the night and into the next day. With a two-day fast like this, the main idea is to get through the first night from six to nine. If you can fill up your time with something during those hours, I've found it so much easier.

For twenty years, I sought to eat on Monday night with my family and fast from Tuesday into Wednesday, finally breaking my fast on Wednesday afternoon or evening. Also, on Tuesday and Wednesday, I would spend more time in prayer. As long as I could get through that six to nine at night block on Tuesday night, I was good.

There were times, however, that I didn't do well during that window. One of my daughters, for example, wouldn't eat that much at dinner, and the rest of her meal found its way into my mouth, or I would take a handful of Cheez-Its and let them serve as communion ☺. At such times, I want to encourage you not to beat yourself up. Let these times serve as reminders of what to watch out for in the future.

Honestly, the main goal is to maintain a spirit of fasting, and sometimes a spoonful of peanut butter or handful of crackers will help take the edge off of your hunger while allowing you to stay in the spirit of fasting. That's the goal.

In addition to the weekly fast, I recommend a three-day monthly fast. In February 2002, the Lord spoke to Mike Bickle of the International House of Prayer in Kansas City (IHOPKC) about fasting for the Bridegroom (see Matt. 9:15). The Lord called Mike to call the Body of Christ to fast the first Monday through Wednesday of every month until He returns. The Lord told Mike to call it "The Global Bridegroom Fast."

Mike said he believed this fast would be one of the most important things he would ever do in his ministry. Over the last seventeen years, I've seen firsthand the power and grace that God has released on these three-day fasts.

VALUE 3: PRAYING IN TONGUES

I cannot even begin to express how valuable extended times of praying in the Spirit have been to my spiritual development. In my opinion, that which the devil has fought overtime to keep the Church from is one of the primary keys that will bring us into maturity, authority, and unity.

We must give ourselves to the practice of praying in tongues for extended periods of time. In a generation that is so "politically correct," we need to be people who will stand for what the Bible says about the glorious gift of praying in the Spirit.

In First Corinthians 1:27-29, Paul wrote, *"God has chosen the foolish things of the world to put to shame the wise, and God has chosen the weak things of the world to put to shame the things*

of which are mighty . . . that no flesh should glory in His presence."
I can't think of a more appropriate application of this than the
phenomena of tongues.

I would not be the person I am today in God and in life
without this glorious gift, and I believe God wants to restore it
in practical application all over the earth.

I've found that twenty to thirty minutes of praying in
tongues in one setting proves to be the catalyst that keeps me
in the spirit of prayer for the rest of the day. In fact, over the
last twenty years, the first fifteen minutes or so of praying in
tongues are filled with a lot of distractions, wandering thoughts,
and emotions, but I've found that, as long as I keep bringing
my mind and focus to God on the throne and His living in
my spirit, my reach for God moves into a divine alignment and
unity with the Spirit of God at the twenty-minute mark.

At twenty minutes, I move into a place where His thoughts
become mine, His prayers become mine, and I begin to see and
believe for God's activity in my life and in the lives of others.
It's at this point where Bible verses begin to pop into my mind
and heart.

Paul laid out many benefits of praying in tongues in his letter
to the Corinthians. I've found these benefits in my own life.

1. Praying in tongues brings me into a direct connection to God.

My spirit and the Spirit of God are one spirit, and as I
begin to pray in the Spirit, I have full confidence that I'm
speaking right to the heart of God. This is a place of deep

intimacy and communion as I pour out my heart before God in tongues.

2. Praying in tongues brings the Spirit of Revelation, which brings understanding of mysteries.

The secret things of God, of me, and of others become known as I pray in tongues. Bible verses become clear. I can hear God's still small voice more clearly, and I begin to "know" things that I had never thought of previously. I attribute these things to the extended time of praying in the Spirit.

3. Praying in tongues strengthens my inner man.

I would say this has been the most frequent benefit that I've found through praying in tongues. My spirit man is strengthened in tongues, releasing power to my mind, my emotions, my will, and my body. Divine life touches me in my most weary seasons as I pray in tongues. I mean might has physically entered my body in my hardest seasons as I've prayed in the Spirit.

4. Praying in tongues forms the character of Christ in my soul.

I can say without question that praying in tongues has made me more like Jesus. His love, tenderness, compassion, patience, and gentleness have been formed in me.

5. Praying in tongues is key in spiritual warfare.

Many people don't understand that, in Ephesians 6, when talking about the spiritual armor, Paul commanded us to pray *"always with all prayer and supplication in the Spirit"* (v. 18). I believe the strong spirit wields the sword of the Spirit against the devil's attacks in our lives. I've found praying militantly in tongues has increased the spirit of prayer in my life.

VALUE 4: READING, STUDYING, LOVING, AND MEDITATING ON THE WORD

One of the deepest passions of my life is to impart to you a deep love affair with the Word of God. I long to see a generation finding their number-one source of joy, delight, and entertainment in the Word of God. As Psalm 1:2 says, *"But his delight is in the law of the Lord, and in His law he meditates day and night."* If you fall in love with the Word, you will also want to obey and submit to the Word.

In a generation that is turning away from truth, we desperately need a new breed of believers, leaders, and missionaries to emerge who have deep intimacy and understanding of the Word. We must have both width and depth when it comes to our relationship with God's Word.

Width

I believe in taking a generation on the journey of reading ten chapters a day, beginning in Genesis and including as many Bible studies as can be processed by students, to help lay the storyline of redemption. So many of our Bible studies begin in the New Testament, which I love, but it's like starting a movie or movie series in the middle instead of at the beginning.

We've got to take our time in studying to see the power of the Creation, the pain of the Fall, the promise of the Seed, and then follow through the lives of Abraham, Isaac, and Jacob and the storyline of Israel and her labor to bring forth Messiah. It's so very important to understand the big picture and how we've been grafted into that glorious storyline with the covenants that God made with Abraham and David, seeing them then secured in Jesus.

Rooting ourselves in the Old Testament delivers us gentiles from notions of arrogance, independence, and isolation. It rightfully postures us with gratitude and humility. It can then move us into intercession for Israel's salvation. In the same way God came to a people who weren't looking for Him—namely, us—so He is going to reveal Himself to a nation that did not recognize His first coming and, consequently, rejected Him.

By having the proper Old Testament foundation, we can feel the appropriate weight on the Word becoming flesh and dwelling among us (see John 1:14). We behold Jesus with different eyes, hear His words with different ears, and tremble with greater awe as Yahweh steps down and takes on our form, emptying Himself of all His divine privileges and hungers. We recognize Him as One who sleeps, endures, prays, groans, preaches, teaches, heals, and delivers. We witness His being ridiculed, beaten, bruised, and hung on a cross. We see Him as He dies, resurrects, ascends, enters into intercession, and returns, rapturing the saints, saving Israel, and ruling the nations from His holy hill in Jerusalem!

I pray that you would come into the story instead of merely reading its scenes. *God, I pray for a breed of believers who love the Word, honor the Word, obey the Word, preach the Word, and impart a love affair with the Word to those who are around them.*

Depth

While I call you to know the story, I also want you to know how and when to slow down, put your Bible down, and let words, phrases, verses, and chapters take you into holy contemplation, meditation, and prayer. I've found that an enflamed heart guards an expanded mind.

If our understanding and clarity of theology doesn't produce more fascination, wonder, tears, and worship, then we are on a slippery slope. My good friend Allen Hood says, "If our minds grow faster than our hearts, we lose discernment."

We need enflamed hearts in love *and* expanded minds in understanding and clarity of Scripture. Some seasons we may focus on one over the other, but we must live in the tension, or we will lose our way.

It's not the information that's going to save the world. It's revelation of the information. My ability to impact others with truth is directly related to the impact that the truth has had on me. Long and loving meditation in the Word of God is the difference maker.

The word that wrecks you with fresh wonder, fascination, and trembling will be the word that changes the world. The most valuable commodity in the whole universe, then, is the Spirit of Revelation resting on you when you read the Word.

VALUE 5: BUILDING A MERCY-BASED CULTURE OF ACCOUNTABILITY

To impact those around us, we must first model vulnerability in our personal lives, weaknesses, and struggles to call them into the same realities.

There have been countless leaders who have fallen in some way because they were alone and the cultures they built did not allow for vulnerability and honesty about personal struggles that would disqualify them. We must build safe, mercy-based cultures of accountability where we share our lives with trusted friends, mentors, and brothers, and where we enter into each other's struggles and contend for break-through in specific areas of weakness.

There are no superheroes who have no weakness; there-fore, we have to remove the paradigm that says Christians, especially Christian leaders, have it all together. We do this by modeling it and inviting it.

I don't believe in telling everyone all our stuff, but I do believe in telling trusted friends, mentors, and brothers or sisters who will walk it out with us as we commit to be honest and vulnerable with them regarding those areas. We need friends who *"love at all times"* and brothers *"born for adversity,"* and we need to be those friends and brothers as well (Prov. 17:17).

One of the most revolutionary things that Jesus did was He called brothers together and sent them out together. I believe the revelation of Jesus as Brother is coming to the Church, and what it's going to do is connect us as men and women to run with other men and women on the mission God has given us in this hour.

So many people are stuck because they are looking for their spiritual father and mother, and I believe wholeheartedly in spiritual parents and mentors. However, I also believe there is a power we haven't considered that's found in the guy or the gal right next to us.

VALUE 6: SLEEPING, EXERCISING, AND RECREATION

The way we rest, exercise, recreate, and eat are all important to our spiritual lives. One of the most overlooked things in our lives is taking seriously the command to keep the sabbath holy. I've done it well in seasons, and in other seasons, I haven't done so well, yet I believe this is key to decades of sustained longevity and fruitfulness.

My ultimate goal is to be burning for God and be as fruitful in my seventies and eighties as I've been in my twenties, thirties, and now forties. We need a marathon mindset to prepare for the long haul and not just a sprint.

We need to ask ourselves about how many hours of sleep we are getting, how many days a week we are working out, and how often we are enjoying some recreation.

How Many Hours of Sleep Are You Getting?

Every person is different. Some people need less sleep than others and can operate at a high level on less sleep;

however, I believe it's healthy to aim for six to eight hours of sleep every night.

God Himself rested, and we must prioritize this to be useful in the coming decades.

In addition to resting nightly, we must rest weekly. I believe in the sabbath rest, but my definition of it may be different than yours. For years, I've made Tuesday my sabbath. It's a day where my prayer hours are longer, my responsibilities are less, and my focus is solely on the Lord.

I also love the day of the week that is family day where we play, rest, and simply enjoy being together. I love these days for football and eating and having fun, but in my mind, it's not my sabbath; it's my family day.

How Many Days a Week Are You Working Out?

One of the most spiritual acts that I've engaged in for the last thirteen years has been working out. There have been some seasons in which I have been faithful to exercise and other seasons I didn't. I've kept swimming upstream, however, to make this a priority.

Nothing clears my mind, reduces my stress, loosens my joints, improves my sleep, and increases my overall productivity like working out. Many people are overweight or out of shape and unable to fulfill the call of God on their lives because of their lack of exercise.

I spent the majority of my twenties just fasting, and then I got into my thirties, and my metabolism started slowing down. The weight started coming on. It was this that caused me to begin to prioritize working out.

One of my goals is to both fast and workout. This is hard because all the people who champion working out don't fast much, and the people who champion fasting don't work out much. We need both, so my encouragement to you is to go on the journey of weekly fasting and weekly working out.

My weekly goal is to exercise in some way three times a week. It has changed from season to season, but my aim is cardio, core, and strength. I currently have a trainer who keeps me accountable to working out because it's so easy to get lost in the mix of life. When I have money invested into something, it changes my approach to it.

How Often Are You Enjoying Some Recreation?

Outside of God, Bible, family, and ministry, I have a deep love for sports. From the time I was five years old to eighteen years old, I had some ball in my hand, so I've always loved watching football and basketball. I think it's healthy for every minister to have something they love to do away from everything else.

My favorite is NBA basketball, and so I try to catch games on TV when I can, and I listen to podcasts on the NBA often. I enjoy this, and I feel the pleasure of God on me when I do.

VALUE 7: PREACHING

I want to talk more about this value in the last section of this book that addresses ways in which we impart the spirit of prayer to others. For now, it's important to realize that all of the values we've discussed should result in the implementation of the value of preaching or sharing what it is we have received. Having ascended the mount of vision, we want to declare what we've seen and heard from that place, and we want to see it reproduced in the lives of others.

My friend, I want to encourage you to just go dig a well! Invest yourself in a consistent lifestyle of prayer, and watch what happens. You'll not only develop a rich history in God, but you will come out with a testimony. That testimony will be so full of the power, authority, and revelation of God that the atmosphere will shift, demons will flee, and lives will be forever changed!

The days of Sunday-only Christianity are coming to a close. Nearness to Jesus is the call and draw of the Spirit. And if you respond to that call and allow Him to create great hunger and lovesickness in your daily life, no longer will anyone have to talk you into prayer, into fasting, or into giving of yourself, your time, your love, or your money.

Why?

Because these will merely be the overflow of the value that His presence is worth everything to you. You won't pray because I told you or because you're supposed to. No, the paradigm will change for you, and like those lovesick disciples of Jesus after He ascended to the Father, you'll run to the secret place, you'll fast, you'll consume His Word—you'll do whatever it takes to be with Him.

6

"PRAY THE LORD OF THE HARVEST"

SOMETHING ELSE HAPPENS TO YOU WHEN THE SPIRIT OF prayer falls on your life as you've developed a life of prayer. Not only does prayer become your inhale and your exhale, as we've discussed in previous chapters, but prayer begins to affect your vision. You start to see things differently. In fact, I believe you begin to see with Jesus' eyes, and what you see and the way you see it will move your heart in a similar way to how Jesus' heart was moved in Matthew 9.

Jesus, in the height of revival, looked back at the crowds that were growing. The people who had been healed, delivered, and set free were grabbing their family and friends and bringing them to Jesus to be touched by Him. It was as if the needs and the demands were exploding all around Him.

In one verse, we are given a rare glimpse into the soul of Jesus Christ. We read, *"But when He saw the multitudes, He was moved with compassion, because they were weary and scattered, like sheep having no shepherd"* (Matt. 9:36).

Apparently, Jesus looked back and *saw* the crowds. He took notice of them. If there is anything that must be restored in this hour in regard to believers and leadership alike is the connection to and unity with Jesus' eyes. To see what He sees—to perceive as He perceives—is a must in this hour.

Jesus looked at the crowds and what He saw moved Him deeply in compassion. His description of the people being like weary and scattered sheep who didn't have a shepherd tells us something. He was pained to see these people exhausted, scattered, and harassed because of the lack of a shepherd or leader.

What Jesus saw was not a people crisis. It was a leader crisis.

In the same way sheep are prone to losing their way and becoming vulnerable to a predator, so these multitudes, if not taken care of, would have become prey to the evil one. Jesus' compassion for them welled up, and He looked for His shepherds to attend to them.

This call for shepherds echoes throughout the Old Testament. God is ever looking for shepherds to lead His people. God prepared Moses to shepherd the nation of Israel out of Egypt by Moses faithfully shepherding his father-in-law's sheep for forty years. David shepherded his father's sheep, thus qualifying him to shepherd the nation of Israel into her greatest hour. The Lord Himself is called the "Shepherd of Israel" in Psalm 80:1. The prophets continually, on the other hand, indicted the leaders of their day over their negligence as shepherds and held them responsible for the state of the people under them (see Jer. 23; Ezek. 34).

The prophet Jeremiah gave us a great promise that, in the last days, God would raise up shepherds according to His heart who would feed people with *"knowledge and understanding of"* Him (Jer. 3:15).

I believe with all my heart that Jesus is once again looking over the earth, and what He is seeing is moving Him to release a deep guttural call across the globe to leaders to connect with His eyes, connect with His heart, and take up the apostolic burden of shepherding the people of God. This is what has pressed me to write this book. I believe you could be one of these shepherds who Jesus is wanting to sweep up into His heart and enable you to see the state of the sheep, giving you a heart full of compassion for them and a shepherding heart to lead them.

Jesus, welling up with holy compassion, grabbed His disciples and brought them into what He was seeing, feeling, and wanting. So, He said to them, *"The harvest truly is plentiful, but the laborers are few. Therefore pray the Lord of the harvest to send out laborers into His harvest"* (Matt. 9:37-38).

Jesus gathered His disciples in closely and in essence told them, "Guys, I want you to see what I see, and I need you to understand that there is not one more thing that needs to be done to prepare this harvest to be reaped. It's here. It's ready. It's plentiful! The issue is not the readiness of the harvest. The issue is that there are few people who know how to reap this harvest and then know what to do with the harvest once they've brought it in. Men, there are few laborers."

This is intense. Just picture Jesus looking at these guys, or make it more personal, picture Him looking at you and me and saying, "You ain't got what it takes to do anything about this." I cannot overstate how hearing this from Jesus is the core door into being used by God in the future days. We must feel this sting of not having what it takes before we will ever be useful to God in any capacity. It's the revelation of our inability that causes us to cast ourselves upon Him to be useful to Him and His Kingdom. This must precede any apostolic usefulness in the Kingdom of God. As Art Katz has written,

> To what degree, therefore, must failure precede a true appropriation of one's calling? . . . There is something about failure, especially when it is born out of the best well-meaning intentions to serve God, that does the depth of work in the human soul like nothing else can. ...
>
> ...There is no man more qualified than the one who believes in his deepest heart that he is without qualification. The whole preliminary work of God is to disqualify us before we can be qualified.[8]

Whatever comes out of Jesus' mouth next will let us know what we can do to respond to our inability and what to do with our pain and our burden for the condition of the people we see. What He says next will strike at the heart of the humanistic, current gospel that is being spread all over this nation as well the nations of the earth.

In light of the immediate needs of the people and the lack of quantity and quality of current laborers, Jesus did not tell the disciples to go. He told them to pray!

Today, Jesus is telling us the same thing, "Pray." Prayer isn't laziness, a waste of time, or foolishness. Praying in light of the immediate needs of the people is the apostolic heart, lifestyle, power, and message of the Gospel. It also exposes all the well-meaning intentions of humanity to use and apply our own wisdom, power, and resource.

Merely because we see something that deserves to be rectified is not necessarily a justification to do it. We cannot act in response to need. We pray.

There is nothing more opposed to the purposes of God than the well-meaning intentions men perpetrate in their own human and religious zeal.

PRAY FOR HIM TO SEND WORKERS

Therefore, Jesus tells us, *"Pray the Lord of the harvest to send out laborers into His harvest."* He doesn't tell us to go, or try to fix the problem, or join a missions trip. He tells us specifically to pray to the *"Lord of the harvest."*

Jesus commands us to throw our lives, our pain, and our burdens in prayer upon the One who owns the harvest, loves the harvest, and has died for the harvest. This is the highest response to seeing the needs of the nations. At first, this can feel deflating because, sometimes when we pray, it doesn't feel like we are accomplishing a lot. God has designed it, however, that the apostolic sending and commissioning would come from the apostolic priority of prayer, feeding on the Word, and the Word becoming flesh in us.

I don't want to run past this command too quickly. The verse we've historically turned into a rallying cry to go is actually a rallying cry to pray.

I believe Jesus in His infinite wisdom is touching the deepest qualification for an apostolic messenger: priestliness. The place of waiting on God in prayer is the place where we die to ourselves and where we are transformed into the laborers God calls and anoints. In the place of waiting before God and begging Him to send us out into the harvest field, God makes us the answer to our own prayer by forming us into laborers, into priests with shepherd hearts.

The word *pray* is not a passive twiddling of our thumbs but is an aggressive, desperate begging of God to be useful to Him in the harvest:

- **We pray.** Prioritizing prayer above every other ministry and every attempt to answer the plight of the people is the apostolic call.

- **We pray.** We sit in silence with a Bible and a water bottle and look at the Father who sees in secret. We cultivate a history of looking Him in the eyes, listening to His voice, and talking to Him.

- **We pray.** We learn how to receive His burden, His investment, His pain, His intercession, and His tears, and then we pray in that vein.

- **We pray.** We spend days, weeks, months, and years, pacing back and forth in a room, fellowshipping with the Spirit, and speaking God's Word back to Him.

- **We pray.** We couple it with fasting for days, crying out for the Spirit of Revelation to come.

- **We pray.** We wait and watch for those holy moments when God descends and pulls us into His eternal intercession for salvation of souls and the opening of doors for the Gospel in the nations.

- **We pray.** We spend days, weeks, months, and years, clinging to God as He slowly deconstructs every false identity or definition of success that we built our lives upon. He slowly dismantles the lies associated with our feelings of fear, shame, and rejection—of being overlooked, being forgotten, or being underappreciated. He continually declares the truth of who He is and who we are to Him and in Him.

- **We pray.** When Satan sifts us and we come into the painful realization that we're not as dedicated as we thought we were, we then begin to see how Jesus' prayers for us are the only reason we made it.

- **We pray.** We endure entire seasons when we feel little, sense little, and our words never seem to go anywhere.

- **We pray.** We meditate on Christ, studying His identity, His life, His death, His resurrection, His ascension, His eternal intercession, and His Second Coming.

- **We pray.** We earnestly beg God to use us and thrust us as laborers into the harvest field.

God loves the harvest more than we do. God is more invested into the harvest than we are. Our greatest usefulness to Him is our being conformed to Him.

Jesus is called the "Lord of the harvest." He is the owner of the harvest. He is the One most invested in, pained over, and committed to the harvest. He knows the most effective way to reap the harvest, and He also knows what to do with it once it's been reaped. In His sovereign timing and choosing, He will send forth laborers into His harvest field.

We throw our lives into the furnace of transformation. We throw our lives, our dreams, and our aspirations on Him. We give Him our five loaves and two fish, entreating Him that He would do something with them. "God, can You use me? I'm jacked up, messed up, but I want You and to be used by You." That's our plea.

I tell you, friend, that if you can get to this point of desperation and humility, you will be useful to Him.

The expression *send forth* (*ekballo*)—as in *"send out laborers"*—is the same expression that is used for casting out demons. Jesus is telling us that, in the same power and force that demons are cast or thrust out, God will show up in places all over the earth in His timing and choosing, and He will thrust forth laborers into the harvest field across the earth.

Jesus declared, *"This gospel of the kingdom will be preached in all the world as a witness to all nations, and then the end will come"* (Matt. 24:14).

I believe God is building wineskins—houses and churches—of prayer across the earth to serve as "greenhouses" for these laborers. This will set the stage for the greatest thrusting forth of apostolic missions in the earth. This will prepare the nations for the greatest and most terrifying hour of human history that will culminate in the return of our Lord and Savior Jesus Christ. Therefore, these messengers must be prepared and trained.

I'm burdened that the kind of preachers and leaders that are graduating from our seminaries and emerging with the largest platforms and churches are simply not equipped to handle the glory and shaking that is scheduled for the earth.

In the same way the elite of the armed forces must undergo the most rigorous training, I believe God is calling us to the prayer rooms to be trained in a specific way that will birth us into the life and spirit of prayer, and the Word of God will be written inside our hearts.

We must return to the ancient paths of God calling His messengers out of prayer rooms instead of only classrooms.

Messengers from those prayer rooms will see as Jesus sees, their hearts will be transformed into the likeness of the Shepherd of Israel, they will be moved just as He is moved, and then they will be thrust into the harvest field as laborers for Him.

IMPARTING THE
SPIRIT OF PRAYER

7

FRIENDS OF THE BRIDEGROOM

FOR THE MAJORITY OF 2019, I CONTINUALLY HEARD THE Holy Spirit shout to me, "Wineskins are changing." No doubt, the Church is in a time of transition for there is a radical shift that is happening throughout the earth. The Lord is preparing His Church for His Second Coming. As a result, prayer meetings are being birthed around the globe.

As we discussed in the previous section, Jesus is taking us to the prayer rooms to teach us what to pray and how to pray. He is wrecking our misconceptions about prayer. And He is changing our paradigms on prayer until our hearts are on fire for His presence, power, glory, and proximity. God is releasing this new paradigm of Himself as our Bridegroom.

ANNOUNCING A NEW PARADIGM

In Matthew 9, we witness an exchange between Jesus and John's disciples. John's disciples came to Jesus and asked,

"Why do we and the Pharisees fast often, but Your disciples do not fast?" (Matt. 9:14). Apparently, John's disciples noticed Jesus' disciples weren't doing the one thing that they thought legitimized their pursuit and practice. It was as if John's disciples were saying, "You don't look like God-chasers in the way we define them. You're not radical like us. Why aren't you radical like us?"

Jesus answered John's disciples with His own question, *"Can the friends of the bridegroom mourn as long as the bridegroom is with them?"* (Matt. 9:15). And then, without waiting for their reply, He said,

> But the days will come when the bridegroom will be taken away from them, and then they will fast. No one puts a piece of unshrunk cloth on an old garment; for the patch pulls away from the garment, and the tear is made worse. Nor do they put new wine into old wineskins, or else the wineskins break, the wine is spilled, and the wineskins are ruined. But they put new wine into new wineskins, and both are preserved (Matthew 9:15-17).

What did unshrunk cloth on an old garment or new wine in old wineskins have to do with Jesus' disciples not fasting? What was Jesus saying to John's disciples?

If I were to use my own words to convey Jesus' response and get to the heart of His message, it would sound something like this, "You don't understand what I'm doing here. I'm introducing an entirely new paradigm of what it means to go after Me—to go after God. It's not based on the Old

Testament way of your doing things to get My attention. No, it's completely different.

"For three and a half years, I'm going to walk, talk, eat, pray, heal the sick, and raise the dead with these disciples of Mine right there with Me. They're going to be so used to proximity with Me that, when I'm taken away from them, they will be cut to the heart. Their hearts will be laid open, and they won't do spiritual disciplines—fasting, prayer, and the like—to get My attention. No, that's not going to be the motivation for their fasting. What will be is lovesickness. They will be so sick with love for Me and My presence that they will mourn and fast for Me and for My return—the return of their Bridegroom."

Jesus was letting John's disciples know that, for a season, He had one agenda, and that was for His disciples to rest in His presence and His nearness. He wanted His own disciples to get used to having Him very near because the days were coming when He would be taken away from them (through His death, resurrection, and ascension) and they would no longer have Him present in Person. According to Jesus, His absence would bring upon His disciples such a deep sense of mourning and longing that then they would fast.

I love Jesus' confidence in His leadership—that the everyday proximity with Him would later produce spiritual longing in His disciples after His absence.

Jesus took this a step further by stating, you don't put the new on the old because the old can't contain or handle the new. Whether it's new patches or new wine, you can't just add it onto old realities because you will lose everything. You need new garments and new wineskins to contain the new patch and new wine respectively!

Jesus was telling them that He was ushering in the new structure, and it didn't look like anything they had seen before. It would not be based on religious duty and obedience but on longing for Him.

This is absolutely revolutionary to us today because it turns everything we know on its head—everything we know and have been taught on spiritual disciplines and what holiness is all about.

I believe with all my heart that what Jesus highlighted here in Matthew 9:15-17 is what the Holy Spirit is doing across the earth with local churches right now. We are in the middle of an extreme home makeover in the local church, and it's God preparing us for the new thing He is about to do.

What exactly is He doing?

Jesus is being brought back to the center. He is becoming to us who He is supposed to be to us: the passion of our hearts, the center of our lives, and the betrothed Bridegroom who is coming back for us.

It means that Sunday-only Christianity is coming to an end. Jesus never meant for His Church to be built around some religious to-do list where we say, "Went to church Sunday, check. Put a twenty in the offering, check. Said a prayer before I went to bed, check." No, that's not what Jesus died for—our forty-five-minute Sunday services and twenty-dollar offerings and two-minute evening prayers.

Prayer rooms are being placed at the heart of local churches, and it's beginning to stoke hunger and thirst for the presence of Jesus. As the appetite increases, the longing for Him increases exponentially.

I believe the local churches that hear what the Spirit is saying and cooperate with what He is doing will move into this next season with apostolic government, resource, wisdom, and strategy. They will move with Jesus into this next season and be entrusted with intimacy, authority, and impact.

The ones who refuse will begin to experience the dimming of their lamps and will lose the influence and impact they currently have, becoming of no use to the Kingdom in the next season.

The revelation of Jesus as Bridegroom is at the heart of this structural change because we aren't just workers, working for our Boss. We are friends of the Bridegroom, laboring with our Bridegroom. This aspect of God refers to His mind, heart, and activity as a Bridegroom. He is a God of covenant. He is a tender, kind, patient Bridegroom. He is a God who pursues us, who desires us. He is a jealous Bridegroom who will not share us with anyone. He is a Bridegroom who tenderly speaks to the budding virtues in our lives until they come into full bloom. He is the One who *"calls those things which do not exist as though they did"* (Rom. 4:17). He suffers long. His love endures.

As we connect to this foundational revelation of God, Christianity will change from "Do I have to?" to "I get to."

I remember in 2001 when the phrase, *"Father, I desire,"* of John 17:24 jumped off the page, and my life was never the same again. The truth that God has desire consumed me and changed everything. He wants me to be with Him where He is, beholding His glory. He's not a stoic, detached, emotionless God, but He is a God of deep desire specifically for me. He desires you, too!

Though I used to try to convince Him to accept me because I was doing all the right things, now I'm understanding that He's trying to awaken me to the dream that has burned in His heart from before the foundation of the world—the dream of His Bride.

MOURNING FOR THE BRIDEGROOM

While John's disciples asked about *fasting,* Jesus spoke about *mourning.* To them, fasting was about discipline. To Jesus, the motivation for fasting, prayer, and all the other spiritual disciplines was mourning.

I believe longing, aching, missing, and groaning are going to lay hold of the Church in a powerful way in the coming days. In the simplest terms, this mourning is the spirit of prayer.

When mourning touches your spirit, you are the most blessed among people. There is no greater gift that God can give to the human spirit than the deep awareness of the gap between Him and us. Jesus in the Sermon on the Mount said, *"Blessed are those who mourn for they shall be comforted"* (Matt.

5:4). While we rest in what we've been brought into, we instinctively know that there is more. This is called *mourning*.

We live in a world that gives us as many options as possible to anesthetize, medicate, and silence our mourning, and sadly, many Christians have said yes to the forbidden fruit in the garden of their souls. Overindulgence in food, entertainment, relationships, and busyness drowns out the groan, and we are left with a form of Christianity that is based on to-do lists that try to keep us in good with God, thereby missing the whole point: Him.

I've done it. You've done it. We've all been guilty of listening to the voice of the enemy who wants us to settle for a lesser form of Christianity that is built around the to-do list versus the get-to opportunities.

This is the new wineskin that is going to prepare the Church for the days ahead of great glory and shaking. We desperately need friends of the Bridegroom in the Body of Christ who will feed the Bride on who she is and who the Bridegroom is, prioritizing ministry to Him above every other ministry.

JOHN'S MINDSET

I believe one of the clearest models of the type of leadership that God will raise up before His return is found in the life and ministry of John the Baptist. In John 3, John's disciples were hearing that Jesus' baptism ministry was becoming bigger than John's. His disciples felt threatened by the fact that this Other Guy's ministry was becoming bigger while

John's ministry was growing smaller. John's answer in John 3:27-30 is the clearest picture of what God is looking for in leaders:

> John answered and said, "A man can receive nothing unless it's been given to him from heaven. You yourselves bear me witness, that I said, 'I am not the Christ,' but 'I have been sent before Him.' He who has the bride is the bridegroom; but the friend of the bridegroom, who stands and hears him, rejoices greatly because of the bridegroom's voice. Therefore, this joy of mine is fulfilled. He must increase, but I must decrease."

John's response to his disciples is unparalleled. I believe contained within John's response is the greatest mindset and revelation needed for leadership in the Body of Christ. It's the lack of this mindset that could likely be one of the greatest hindrances to the outpouring of the Holy Spirit and maturation of the Church. A man or woman who can answer this question in the way John did has been formed in a specific place: the wilderness of prayer and fasting. This is the *only* place where such a mindset is formed.

John's line, "*A man can receive nothing unless it's been given to him from heaven,*" is the most freeing statement for any leader in any sphere anywhere.

Why?

Because, if you can say that out of conviction, then you understand there is no person, there is no devil, there is no one and nothing that can take anything from you if God has ordained for you to have it. John understood this.

What would happen if every pastor in America thought this way?

Revival would happen.

When leaders do not have John's mindset, then everyone is seen as a threat. When leaders are suspicious of the threat of others, they guard, protect, manipulate, and control everyone and everything in "their" sphere so as to not be harmed or negatively affected.

There have been many times in my life where I've been overlooked, not seen, spoken of in a wrong way, or limited by the closing of a door of opportunity for me. Time and time again, I've seen God turn the whole thing around and open the door He wanted me to walk through. No one ever stopped me from going through the doors He has opened for me.

I know what it feels like to have a leader see me in a limited light. It was this verse that I clung to in those times because I knew no one could stop what God had ordained for me. I also understood that I could not make happen what God had said no to. It was this verse that freed me from the temptation to defend myself, fight for myself, or make room for myself.

I've felt the temptation before, and I've seen many people seek to use their proximity to a leader or their connections to "open a door" of opportunity. Sadly, I've seen those same people succeed in getting that position or that conference or that ministry opportunity. To work so hard to open a door that you don't have the call and the anointing to walk through is one of the most terrifying things to me in the world. There is nothing worse than being the only person in the room who doesn't recognize how you are not called and anointed to be in the place where you used your own strength to get you there.

Mike Bickle shared, in my opinion, one of the greatest stories of something that happened to him regarding control and manipulation. He was doing a series of meetings in the United Kingdom. Before one of the meetings, he was praying in his hotel room. (He would minister to five thousand pastors later that evening.) The Holy Spirit began to tell him, "I have a controversy with the leadership of this nation. No one with a control spirit will experience My power."

Mike began to tell the Lord, "God, I'm in the middle of a controversy—"

Interrupting him, the Lord said, "I'm in a controversy!"

Mike understood by the Lord's statement that he was to share what the Lord had told Him in the first place.

Later that evening, Mike preached his message, and then for the altar call, with his head down, he began to whisper, "The Lord has a controversy with the leaders of this nation, and no one with a control spirit will experience His power."

In his own testimony about that night, he shared that, after he said what God had told Him to say a couple of times, one by one, pastors began to shoot to the ground. Before he knew it, hundreds of pastors began to writhe on the ground like snakes as demons began to come out of them. It was the most supernatural work of the Holy Spirit that he had ever seen, and it was around the Lord's zeal to confront and deliver His leaders from control and manipulation.

THE BRIDEGROOM HAS THE BRIDE

I believe with all my heart that the revelations John high-lighted will become the core realities of messengers in the coming days. He made it very clear that the people he was baptizing, the people who were listening to his messages and the nation of Israel as a whole, were not "his" in any sense of the word. They were the Bride, and they belonged to the Bridegroom and not him.

One of the most crucial understandings that leaders must gain in these days is that we are stewarding another Man's wife. Our call as leaders is not to draw her to us, our gift-ings, or our abilities, but to introduce her to the One who purchased her with His royal blood: Jesus. We must prepare her for her wedding day to her Bridegroom by proclaiming His heart, His zeal, His tenderness, His covenant, and His longing for her. We must proclaim the "why" of the cross in addition to the "what" of the cross.

God is a Bridegroom. This may be the first time that you have ever heard of this, but it's true. From Genesis to Revelation, it is very clear that God is a Bridegroom. The Bible begins with a wedding, and it ends with a wedding. From the very beginning when Eve was taken from Adam's side and presented to Adam, we know that this was a picture of Christ and the Church.

Mount Sinai was a betrothal ceremony as God betrothed Himself to the nation of Israel. This is why the prophets called Israel's idolatry *harlotry*. This is why Hosea married a prostitute and kept pursuing her, because this is what was going on with God toward Israel.

Jeremiah called the nation back to the Bridegroom (see Jer. 3).

Isaiah proclaimed, *"For your Maker is your husband, the Lord of hosts is His name"* (Isa. 54:5). And he said, *"As the bridegroom rejoices over the bride, so shall your God rejoice over you"* (62:5).

Song of Solomon highlights the ecstasy of marital love but is also an allegory of the love of Christ for the Church.

Jesus' first miracle was at a wedding (see John 2:6-10).

Jesus called Himself *the Bridegroom*.

He called His disciples *friends of the Bridegroom*.

John called himself *the friend of the Bridegroom*.

Matthew 22:2 states the Kingdom of Heaven is like a wedding that the Father prepared for His Son.

Matthew 25:1-4 states the Kingdom of Heaven is like five wise and five foolish virgins preparing for a wedding.

Revelation 19:7 thunders, *"Let us be glad and rejoice and give Him glory, for the marriage of the Lamb has come, and His wife has made herself ready"*!

The name of the New Jerusalem is *the Bride* (see Rev. 21:2).

I could go on and on about the continual use of this paradigm in Scripture. It's not a side issue, a weird issue, or an extra issue, but it is a central paradigm that leaders must come into so as to partner with God's heart and plan in these last days.

THE FRIEND OF THE BRIDEGROOM STANDS AND HEARS HIM

John then, in rare form, gave definition to who he was and what his job description was. He was the friend of the Bridegroom whose primary occupation was standing before God and hearing Him.

This standing and hearing invoked the priestly language of standing before the Lord. John was making it clear that his job was as a priest who stood before the Lord and heard His voice. I have no doubt that John had encounters with the Lord during those years in the wilderness, but hearing the Voice was primarily done by hearing the Bridegroom through the pages of the Old Testament.

Once again, I believe that the most crucial call to spiritual leadership in the earth is the cultivation of a history of ministering to the Lord and encountering Him as the Bridegroom.

It's not preaching. Not teaching. Not counseling. It's standing and hearing.

I cannot help but think here of Acts 6 and the apostles as they came to the conclusion that they must give themselves *"continually to prayer and to the ministry of the word"* (v. 4).

THE FRIEND OF THE BRIDEGROOM REJOICES

Outside of Jesus, John the Baptist was the happiest man that ever lived because he derived his joy from encountering the Bridegroom. John's joy and success did not come from how big the crowds were who came to him, how much money he had, or how great his following was. John's joy stemmed from hearing Jesus' voice.

John's definition of success was encountering Jesus.

John's definition of success was hearing Jesus.

The fulfillment of joy was in John's encounter with Jesus. Nothing could add to or take away from John's joy because of how he defined success.

If you will find your success and highest joy in encountering Jesus and His voice, you will become one of the most dangerous people who ever lived. You will unnerve every religious spirit, political spirit, networking spirit, and spirit of control and manipulation because you can't be bought, controlled, or manipulated by money, opportunities, applause, or open doors.

Others won't be able to touch you or maneuver you because your reward won't be found in something someone can give you or take away from you.

We are so familiar with John's statement, *"He must increase, but I must decrease,"* but do we understand that this statement comes from a heart rooted in the superior joy of hearing the Bridegroom's voice?

The thing that separates John from everybody else is that he prepared his whole life for a six- to eighteen-month ministry. As soon as Jesus showed up, John gladly and willingly gave up his ministry as he pointed everyone to Jesus. He didn't hold onto "his" ministry because "his ministry" was standing and hearing, not "standing and preaching."

We all want Jesus to increase as we decrease, but unless our joy is in Him and in encountering His Word, we will not decrease when He calls us to. This will become a painful process as He pulls from our hands the things we were never called to hold onto.

My prayer is that God would raise up one hundred thousand leaders across the earth who are friends of the Bridegroom and whose sole ambition is encountering Him and His voice. My heart is that He would restore the priestly ministry of standing and rejoicing in hearing Him.

8

PREACHING: STEWARDING A BURDEN

IF YOU'LL RECALL IN CHAPTER 5, WE IDENTIFIED SEVEN values that we should apply to our lives when creating a consistent life of prayer. The seventh value we briefly looked at was preaching. I've always viewed preaching as an extension of the spirit of prayer. It's what happens out of the overflow of divine encounter with God. Something that I tell people often is that I never go to the Bible to find a message to preach. My goal is not preaching. It's connection with God and His heart and His Word. As I build a life of prayer and pursue His heart, He fills me with Him, and out of the overflow of that encounter, I spill over into imparting that to others through preaching.

The four living creatures are night-and-day preachers of the "holy, holy, holy," and yet their message comes out of who it is they have been staring at. In many ways, they are my model as a preacher. Their focus is on God—not on themselves and their articulation or their wisdom or nuance. They're fascinated with God!

One of my greatest pains is the emphasis on human wisdom, articulation, and attractive presentation in so much of our modern-day preaching. We desperately need fresh throne-room encounters to expose and awaken our messengers in these days.

In Isaiah 6:1, Isaiah saw the Lord *"high and lifted up, and the train of His robe filled the temple."* He then heard seraphim, singing to one another, *"Holy, holy, holy . . . the whole earth is full of His glory"* (v. 3). When Isaiah heard the undefiled song of the angels in Heaven, he got exposed, *"Woe is me, for I am undone! Because I am a man of unclean lips . . . for my eyes have seen the King, the Lord of hosts"* (v. 5).

Isaiah's lips got exposed when his eyes got opened. There is a direct connection between the eyes being opened and the lips getting exposed. When Isaiah heard those angels sing, he then realized in essence, "I don't know who I'm talking about." He had a prophetic ministry, yet he realized the shallowness and emptiness of his message because it was devoid of encounter.

I have one obsession in this life, and it's an obsession for the Spirit of Revelation. I am a treasure hunter in search of facets of the beauty of Jesus to strike my heart, release fresh tears, and awaken fresh worship in my heart.

I included this chapter in this book because I believe we need a whole new breed of preachers who, at the core, are worship leaders. They preach from that mount of divine vision because of whom they have built their lives around.

It's this kind of prophetic preaching that carries unction, authority, and conviction—preaching that cuts through the noise and confusion of the culture and our present pulpits.

One of the greatest dreams of my life is to see an army of prophetic preachers arise across the globe. I want to see preachers like John the Baptist who will thunder the glory of Christ and His coming. Friend, I want to see you become one of those messengers, one of those communicators who manifest the Word and God's heart for people.

Whether you speak to one, ten, one hundred, one thousand, or ten thousand, it doesn't matter. God controls the sphere of influence. Our call is to cultivate the reality and authenticity of what we say when we say it.

In the same way that I wrote on how the spirit of prayer falls on the life of prayer, so I believe that God wants to train us to take something we've discovered as we've gazed on Him through a process and bring forth a message that releases Heaven into Earth.

I have been preaching many times a week for nearly twenty years, and I have discovered a path that I believe can take you from your encounter in God through the Word and the Spirit to holy words that break through to the human heart.

I want to take you on a journey on how God takes me from seeing something in the Word under the Spirit of Revelation to becoming something that God wants me to speak.

THE BURDEN

I've often been asked, "How do you know if or when God is highlighting something in the Word?" I think the simple answer to this question is you know God is highlighting something when the words you're reading seem to come at you in a way you've never seen them before. Along with that, I usually experience a feeling or sense that there's something significant or even prophetic about what I'm seeing. Something will stand out of the passage which will create a new question or new insight. If stewarded well, this whisper can become a roar to shift people for eternity.

When God begins to rest on a specific theme or chapter or verse, it's at this point that I will begin to slow down and shift into a different mode. I will familiarize myself with the chapters and verses surrounding the one I feel the Lord is highlighting. I will also become familiar with the context of the original audience.

Slowly, I will read the portion of text over and over again. I will intermingle times of writing notes, highlighting repetitive words and phrases, with prayer, asking the Holy Spirit to show me what I need to see in the passage.

This place of divine fascination around revelation must become your reward. Just as John said he rejoiced in hearing God's voice, so should you. Thank Him for opening up your understanding and revealing His heart about the Word. Rejoice in it!

My goal is not a message, a book, a song, a social media post, or something cool to share with someone. My goal is simply encountering Him.

As I've said, I've never gone to the Word for a message. In the midst of my love affair with the Word, messages emerge and grow. I believe it's dangerous in the long run to "try" to get messages.

There is a fourfold process that I follow when I begin to feel God birthing a message in me. This process is widely used among popular preachers.

1. Read yourself full.

2. Think yourself clear.

3. Pray yourself hot.

4. Let yourself go!

READ YOURSELF FULL AND THINK YOURSELF CLEAR

This process can sometimes take up to six months as I marinate, saturate, memorize, visualize, contemplate, and meditate in these passages. This is my favorite part of the process because I'm seeing God in a way that I've never seen Him before and feeling Him in a new way as well.

I will read and reread the same passage over and over again. I will speak in tongues during my memorization of the passage so I can walk and pace and speak the phrases back to God. Extended hours in prayer increase revelation as well.

The majority of my reading and thinking comes from the Word of God and what I see in Scripture, but I will use books and commentaries to support what God is saying to me and doing in me.

Several years ago, the revelation of the shepherd's rod out of Psalm 23 was really impacting me. It was in that season of continual meditation in Psalm 23, Hebrews 12, and the discipline of the Lord that I read Bob Sorge's book *The Chastening of the Lord.*

This book brought a lot of clarity to me on the subject, and it also confirmed much of what God was already telling me in my private study and meditation. So many phrases from Bob's book resonated deeply and gave language to some of the roadblocks I was having in processing how to say certain realities. It literally gave me words for some of my unexpressed thoughts.

I will also use commentaries. The commentaries will help with historical context and help with some of the words in Greek and Hebrew, thus broadening my understanding of the passage. I'm very careful, however, to lean more on the Word and the Holy Spirit. We need to allow the Word to interpret the passage as well as listen to what the Holy Spirit has to say about it.

I truly lean on the passage in First John 2 where we are told that we have the anointing that teaches us *"concerning all things"* (v. 27). We each have an anointing, and as we learn to honor the anointing and give way to the anointing, clarity and the true heart of the passage will surface into our understanding.

I believe in the anointing of God on my life and in my life to teach me and to bring forth the true heart and message of the passage. I pull on the anointing during this season.

I remember Mike Bickle saying one time, "Study your anointing." What he meant by that is to learn the way God moves in your life and brings you into a passage or into how He uses you. God has tailor-made ways with each of us. It would do us all well to familiarize ourselves with them.

During my study of the passage, I begin to employ the power of questions. I've found that questions are the doorway into revelation. Some of the questions seem to surface naturally. For example, I may ask:

- What face of Jesus is being emphasized in the passage?

- What issue is being confronted in me?

- What is the bottom-line message of the passage?

I wrestle over these questions as I sit before the Word, and I'll wait until clarity comes. Friend, don't be unnerved by the process of time. The confusion and fog will lift if you just stay before God in the Word.

Toward the end of reading yourself full, you will move into thinking yourself clear. I usually keep a journal with me to make note of what I'm hearing. In it, I will write down my thoughts, other Scriptures, rough outlines, or the passage itself. Writing and clear thinking go hand in hand.

Furthermore, I will type notes on my computer and begin to think about the flow of the message. A lot of people don't know this about me, but the notes of almost every message that I preach are typed and stored on my computer. Some people may look at my style of delivery and call it spontaneous or say I'm flying by the seat of my pants, but I'm very rigorous in preparing a message, the flow of it, the construction of it, and the outlining of it.

Preaching the Word of God is the highest honor in the world. It is not a small thing that we do. You are speaking on behalf of our glorious God, and it is not a light matter. Eternity hangs in the balance. Souls hang in the balance. Destinies hang in the balance.

For one short moment in time, my path will cross with another person's path, and in that encounter, there is the possibility for something to be said or happen that will change the person forever. Because of that, I must do my due diligence in preparing myself and the message through the rigorous scrutiny of the life I live and the message I preach.

I will spend months wrestling over verses, praying through verses, speaking verses until clarity comes inside me. I will wrestle over every phrase, every story—everything! I believe this is what Paul was describing when he wrote Timothy and said, *"Be diligent to present yourself approved to God, a worker who does not need to be ashamed, rightly dividing the word of truth"* (2 Tim. 2:15).

We need a new generation of preachers who are diligent to be approved by God. If I'm approved by God, I can handle being rejected by men. When you are approved by God in preparation and preaching, you are not ashamed, and you can stand confidently, knowing you pleased the Father regardless of how the crowd responds.

So, while typing my message, I will speak the passage over and over in my mind and pray into the flow of the message. I will then begin to move into articulation to God, myself, and others.

As a preacher, I'm constantly looking for ways to say something that encapsulates the full thought. One of the ways that has helped me in communication is Twitter. Twitter forces me into employing only 130 characters to say what it is I need to say. It presses me to say what I'm sensing in a concise way.

At the end of the day, people will remember statements more than they will remember messages. They will even remember sentences more than books.

I will also do short videos on Instagram, giving little snippets of what I'm feeling or seeing from the passage. I will do this to get it out as well as see if or how it lands with people. I will ask myself more questions like:

- Does what I say make sense?
- Does it communicate to the week-old believer as well as the thirty-year-old saint?
- Does it empower the weakest believer bound in shame and fear as well as the deepest, godliest person who is mature?

- Is my truth filled with grace, and is my grace filled with truth?

- Does it provoke?

- Does it provide the remedy?

My ultimate desire as a preacher is to help take deep theological truths and use common language as bridges to provoke and equip people to grow in the reality I'm sharing.

My objective is not only to help them understand, however; it's also to break up the fallow ground of their hearts, helping escort them into fascination and wonder and worship.

There have been many times in my life where I preached and didn't sense the breakthrough or didn't feel that my words hit the mark, or that the message was received. After all of my swirl in it, I'll go to the Father and ask Him, "What did You think about it?"

Amazingly, He will often just say, "You did so good, son."

That whisper settles my soul and dispels a thousand fears, insecurities, and lies that had come against me.

We need a new generation of messengers who will not bow to the people, or the wants and desires of the people, but who will preach the Word. We need Bible preaching and teaching—not just cool stories.

The apostle Paul said it best when addressing Timothy, his son in the faith:

> *I charge you therefore before God and the Lord Jesus Christ, who will judge the living and the dead at*

His appearing and His kingdom: Preach the word!
Be ready in season and out of season. Convince,
rebuke, exhort, with all longsuffering and teaching.
For the time will come when they will not endure
sound doctrine, but according to their own desires,
because they have itching ears, they will heap up for
themselves teachers; and they will turn their ears
away from the truth, and be turned aside to fables.
But you be watchful in all things, endure afflictions,
do the work of an evangelist, fulfill your ministry
(2 Timothy 4:1-5).

PRAY YOURSELF HOT AND LET YOURSELF GO

Pray yourself hot refers to the minutes, hours, and days leading up to your message during which you pray, fast, and ask God for His fire and anointing to fall on the message.

I will take my notes and print them out. During the days prior to my sharing the message, I take those notes and memorize them, pacing back and forth and hearing myself speak my notes aloud. I will say the various phrases to myself so that they really get inside me.

I specifically engage in hours of speaking in tongues preceding a message. My desire is to get the information from the notes and Word, and get them into my spirit because, at the end of the day, I long for an impartation to be released through the message that shifts the hearers into the same reality.

I personally believe that praying in the Spirit around the Word releases the Word into your spirit. When it finally is released in its fullness, the Word comes out as a sword that cuts, divides, exposes, and releases power.

Let yourself go refers to the moment you step into the anointing on your life and just go for it, delivering the message you have been carrying. This looks different for everyone and is based on an individual's gifting and calling. This is where you simply be you and not try to be someone else. The anointing flows freely this way.

Young David couldn't wear King Saul's armor to fight Goliath, and neither can you. You must wear your own armor and release the message the Lord has given you, doing so within the call on your life.

God moves on authenticity. Be true to yourself and Him, and He will back you up.

Just like any skill, preaching is developed over time. After twenty years of preaching over two thousand sermons, I truly believe that I'm just starting to hit my stride in clarifying my message, adjusting it to my audience, and moving with the prophetic spirit while staying true to the flow of the message.

Remember the apostle Peter's exhortation, *"If anyone speaks, let him speak as the oracles of God. If anyone ministers, let him do it as with the ability which God supplies, that in all things God may be glorified through Jesus Christ, to whom belong the glory and the dominion forever and ever"* (1 Pet. 4:11).

Preaching is so much more than giving information. It's bringing those who are hungry and willing into an encounter with the living God.

Preaching is an act of intercession as you stand in the gap between God and man in Christ, and help create a meeting place between the two. The words born out of hours of meditation, study, and prayer open up doors for men and women, believer and unbeliever alike, to encounter God.

NUANCES TO PREACHING

There are so many nuances that go into preaching. You can preach the same message using the same verses, and it can come out completely different based on the audience you are speaking to, the culture they live in, how old they are, and what their depth of biblical understanding is. There are so many nuances that are learned through trial and error, and you have to go on the journey to learn what these things are.

I've probably preached Ephesians 1:16-19 over seven hundred times, and I've seen God take that message in at least two hundred different ways. The Lord may highlight the spirit of religion in one setting, the revelation of the Father in another, or the revelation of the Son in yet another. He may even underscore the difference between wisdom and revelation or the power of the eyes at different times among different people. This is just how it goes.

MY FOUR LIFE MESSAGES

Earlier, I encouraged you to study your anointing. When you do this, you may also want to consider what message or messages God seems to be calling and anointing you to preach.

For example, after twenty years of preaching, I've boiled down all of my messages into four categories. Each one of these categories are broad enough to contain many subjects yet specific enough to make me cognizant of what God wants to do through me.

Here is what I believe God has called me the most to live, embody, and proclaim:

1. The knowledge of God
2. Fellowshipping with the Spirit
3. Revelation of intercession
4. Forerunner ministry

These four subject categories represent the deepest longings of my own heart personally as well as my longings for the greater Body of Christ. Here is a list of these four longings, each matching with the respective subject category above:

1. I want to know God deeply and intimately, never settling for yesterday's revelation.
2. I want greater intimacy with the indwelling Spirit.
3. I want the spirit of prayer to rest on my life.
4. I want to be prepared and prepare others for the hour of Christ's return.

Now, if you look at the five books that I've written prior to this one you're now reading, you'll see how they each fit with their respective subject category as well:

1. *Pursuit of the Holy* is my life's cry for the knowledge of God.

2. *Glory Within* is my life's cry for intimacy with the Holy Spirit.

3. *Ancient Paths* falls underneath intimacy with the Holy Spirit.

4. *Prayer* is my life's message on intercession.

5. *Inheritance* proclaims that forerunners must prepare themselves and others for the return of Christ.

I believe it's good to know your life's verses. They keep you anchored and focused. There are even times when fresh fire falls on them and impacts you in a dynamic way. Here are my verses:

1. Ephesians 1:16-19

2. 1 Corinthians 2:9-13

3. Hebrews 7:25

4. Isaiah 40:3

VULNERABILITY AFTER PREACHING

I don't think there is a more physically, mentally, emotionally, and spiritually exhausting labor on the earth like preaching. Charles H. Spurgeon once said, "If any man will preach as He should preach, his work will take more out of him than any other labor under heaven."[9]

I have found that, after some of my greatest and most powerful times of preaching and ministry, I have been the most susceptible to the schemes of the devil. I have had bouts of depression and lust hit me, and I have had to learn how to navigate these swirls. Being poured out over a weekend is exhausting, and if you're not prepared for that, you can get caught off guard. I'm very intentional about my re-entry into home life and prayer life.

The devil roams around looking for *"whom he may devour,"* and he looks specifically for those opportune times of vulnerability to strike at our hearts to disqualify us and disconnect us from our families (1 Pet. 5:8).

I am being very vulnerable with you right now, but one of the things that will hit me when I'm returning from a trip is the fact that I have been gone too much from my wife and kids. If I'm not careful while returning from a trip, I will begin to look and think about the next month or season of travel. I'll find myself getting sad about it and begin to believe the lie that I'm not a good husband or dad. I have spent many return flights home, crying and praying through these swirls.

My wife and kids are very aware of this struggle, and they are amazing at breaking those lies and praying me through while I am away on weekends. My family and I are all in this together, and I'm so grateful for their love and for who they are.

Several things help me when returning from a trip. Everyone is different, and you will just need to learn what works for you, but here is a list of things that seem to help me when returning home:

1. Watching a movie on the plane ride home. Unless I'm caught up with reading a certain book, working on notes for an upcoming session, or writing a book, I will usually download a movie and watch it. This helps me decompress and rest my mind and soul. It also helps me to pass the time as I'm not left to my thoughts and where they could take me.

2. Intimacy with my wife. When I return home, I want to serve my wife by helping around the house and doing anything I can to help relieve the load she has been carrying alone over the weekend. I also long for verbal, emotional, and physical intimacy with my wife. Our kids know that my first night back is for their mom and dad to spend alone time together. This reconnects us and breaks any confusion or separation the enemy wants to insert between us.

3. Connection with my kids. I love to take my kids to breakfast, lunch, or anywhere we can be together. I absolutely love being with my kids, and I want them always to know that my highest joy is being with them. I date all my girls, and they know they are a high priority to me.

4. Early morning prayer. If I return at a decent hour on Sunday night, my aim is to wake up and either go into the prayer room or spend one to two hours in prayer and the Word in my living room. I'm grateful for my wife, kids, and other blessings, but nothing fills the poured-out heart like time with Jesus.

5. Working out. Over the last thirteen years, I have been very intentional in building a regular workout routine. Whether it be cardio, weightlifting, or core stuff, working out helps me clear my mind, reduce my stress, increase my energy, improve my sleep patterns, and re-center me after an intense weekend of ministry. My goal is to be useful to God in my old age, so I must make the necessary investment now.

LAST THOUGHTS ON PREACHING

All preaching, whether from the Old Testament or New Testament, should be filled with Christ and the crucified life, and it should point to Christ and His crucifixion and resurrection. Just as Paul said, *"I determined not to know anything among you except Jesus Christ and Him crucified"* (1 Cor. 2:2).

This doesn't mean that every passage has to have Jesus' name in it, but you should backdrop every passage with a call to Him and the reality of death and then the resurrection.

I promise you that every passage in the Word leads to Him. Don't stop until you find how the present passage that you're studying comes back to Him. We always want to leave Christ and His death and resurrection on the minds and hearts of the people. You want to impart Him, and not yourself, to others.

9

"THE SPIRIT AND THE BRIDE SAY, 'COME!'"

IN ONE OF THE LAST VERSES IN THE BIBLE, WE GET A prophetic picture of what we will look like before our Bridegroom returns. Revelation 22:17 says, *"The Spirit and the bride say, 'Come!'"* In this verse, we see three amazing things that will happen in the Church across the earth.

1. The Holy Spirit and the Church will come into unity.

2. The Church will come into her bridal identity.

3. The spirit of prayer will become the primary anointing.

We are going to see an acceleration of the revelation of Jesus as Bridegroom before He returns, and we are going to see a great longing arise in the Church across the earth for our Bridegroom to return. We will begin to cry out for Him. We will want Him because we've seen Him with the eyes of faith.

As I have said before, I believe we will see Jesus and want Him because end-time messengers will proclaim Him in the same way John did before Jesus came. These friends will introduce the Bride to the Holy Spirit, the ultimate Friend of the Bridegroom. The Holy Spirit will bring the Bride into her bridal identity and anoint her with the spirit of prayer.

We are at the beginning of this revelation coming to the Church, but it's only going to increase. Right now, the cry for Jesus to come is only a whisper, but it will become a roar before He returns.

Most of the Church is content with Jesus staying up there in Heaven and us enjoying life down here, but there is coming a great longing and mourning for the Bridegroom King to return and rule the earth. And the great news is the Church will be glorious before He comes.

The greatest miracle that God will perform in the last days will be taking a Laodicean church filled with the spirit of this age and bring us into a holy Church set on fire. God will take a divided, dull, bored people and will transform us into a Revelation 22:17 Bride who is spotless, holy, united with the Holy Spirit, and anointed with the spirit of prayer. He will *"present her to Himself a glorious church, not having spot or wrinkle or any such thing, but that she should be holy and without blemish"* (Eph. 5:27).

I'm reminded of two portions of Scripture that rejoice my heart about the coming days:

> *"Let us be glad and rejoice and give Him glory, for the marriage of the Lamb has come, and His wife has made herself ready." And to her it was granted to be arrayed in fine linen, clean and bright, for the fine linen is the righteous acts of the saints* (Revelation 19:7-8).
>
> *And on this rock, I will build My church, and the gates of hades will not prevail against it. And I will give you the keys of the kingdom of heaven, and whatever you bind on earth will be bound in heaven, and whatever you loose on earth will be loosed in heaven* (Matthew 16:18-19).

Right now, the Church is bound up in compromise, apathy, and sin. We are bored with Jesus and disconnected from what He is doing in these days, but God is going to change this before His Son returns.

How do I know?

Because Jesus prayed for it, and Jesus gets His prayers answered!

In the High Priestly Prayer, Jesus petitioned the Father:

> *That they all may be one, as You, Father, are in Me, and I in You; that they also may be one in Us, that the world may believe that You sent Me. And the glory which You gave Me I have given them, that they may be one just as We are one: I in them, and*

You in Me; that they may be made perfect in one, and that the world may know that You have sent Me, and have loved them as You have loved Me. Father, I desire that they also whom You gave Me may be with Me where I am, that they may behold My glory which You have given Me; for You loved Me before the foundation of the world. O righteous Father! The world has not known You, but I have known You; and these have known that You sent Me. And I have declared to them Your name, and will declare it, that the love with which You loved Me may be in them, and I in them (John 17:21-26).

The Father will answer this prayer in the Church before Jesus returns. Every phrase of this prayer and every word of this prayer will be answered!

Though I could walk through every phrase of these last six verses, the only one that I want to highlight is verse 22, where Jesus connects the release of glory with our coming into unity. Please understand that unity is not the fruit of "trying harder" and "doing more stuff together," but it includes the release of glory on the end-time Church to come into a quality that is truly the work of God.

No man, church, denomination, or plan will accomplish the unity of John 17. It will be the direct result of "glory." This glory is the end-time outpouring of the Holy Spirit on all flesh across the earth. This glory will bring us where we cannot go outside of Him.

No matter what we as the Church look like today, I tell you, by the prayer of our Lord Jesus Christ, the glorious outpouring of the Spirit will come to pass. In the same way the prayer of Jesus secured this reality, so the prayer of the Church and her leaders will cause it to become reality.

Paul undoubtedly was thinking of John 17 when he wrote to the Ephesian church about the purpose of the fivefold gifting in the Church:

> *And He Himself gave some to be apostles, some prophets, some evangelists, and some pastors and teachers, for the equipping of the saints for the work of ministry, for the edifying of the body of Christ, till we all come to the unity of the faith and of the knowledge of the Son of God, to a perfect man, to the measure of the stature of the fullness of Christ* (Ephesians 4:11-13).

The purpose of fivefold ministries is to strengthen the Body of Christ to the extent that we become unified in the faith and the revelation of Jesus Christ.

God is going to use three things to bring forth a Revelation 22:17 Bride. He's going to use:

1. The global outpouring of the Holy Spirit
2. The Great Tribulation
3. Fivefold ministries

God will use great presence and great pressure to produce great prayer.

I want you to think about how God has brought you to the current place you are in in your life with Him. What process has He used?

For me, it's been presence and pressure. His presence tenderizes me, washes me, renews me, and awakens me to Him and His beauty, but His pressure delivers me, refines me, purifies me, and changes me. His presence and pressure deliver me from doing Christianity in my own strength, wisdom, and gifting. His presence and pressure produce a greater dependence on the Holy Spirit and others.

God will use presence and pressure to deliver us from independence and isolation. Right now, in days of relative peace and safety, we are good with our forty-five minutes and twenty-dollar offerings once a week while living the other six days, twenty-three hours, and fifteen minutes of our week in our little bubbles, occasionally thanking Jesus for His goodness yet living disconnected from Him and each other.

His glory and shaking will spin us off our islands of individualism, and we will find ourselves in prayer rooms and at dinner tables going somewhere together.

God's glory and shaking will drive us into a deeper dependence on the Holy Spirit because the truth is we aren't smart enough or gifted enough. Neither do we have enough resource to navigate increased presence and pressure.

THE REVELATION OF THE HOLY SPIRIT

One of the most critical truths for the end-time Church will be the revelation of the Holy Spirit. In fact, the revelation of the Holy Spirit is going to revolutionize the Church. Right now, we ascribe to Him in theory and doctrine, but our understanding and knowledge of Him are going to become deeply personal before Jesus returns.

For the last two thousand years, the Holy Spirit has been on FM while the Church has been on AM, yet I have no doubt that we will get on the same frequency before the Lord returns.

God is going to use great presence and great pressure to deliver the Church from doing Christianity in her own strength, wisdom, and resource. We will be forced into greater dependency on the Holy Spirit.

Paul told the church in Galatia that they were being *"bewitched"* thinking that, though they had begun in the Spirit, they could be justified and made perfect in the flesh (Gal. 3:1). They had been deceived to think that they could save, redeem, and justify themselves in the flesh.

God has made us a new creation with a new spirit, new identity, new relationship with Him, and new destiny with Him. To turn around and live devoid of an active, continual, deliberate engaging of the Spirit in your journey of maturity and development is impossible. It is impossible for us to mature in God and develop apart from the active work of the Spirit in our lives and our yielded response to it.

Friend, I want you to know that one of the most practical things you can do today to prepare for Christ's coming is to develop a deep history of intimacy with the Holy Spirit.

How much do you talk to the Holy Spirit? How much do you commune and fellowship with Him? Are you even aware of His presence within you?

The more you engage Him, the more a cry will begin to arise within you for His coming because the Holy Spirit is the Spirit of adoption that cries out.

It breaks my heart to see the way that many in the Church treat the Third Person of the Trinity. We've relegated Him to some addendum in the Trinity, but He is God! He is as much God as the Father is God and as Jesus is God.

No one loves Jesus more than the Holy Spirit.

No one knows Jesus more than the Holy Spirit.

No one reveals Jesus except the Holy Spirit.

I'm convinced that most of our minimizing of Him within the Godhead is due to the fact that we can't define and control Him in the same way we can Jesus. What I mean by that is we can read the Gospels and be able to define Jesus (at least we think we can), and this makes us feel safe with Him because He fits within our constructs and boxes.

Most of us feel pretty safe with the Father because Jesus said, when we see Him, we see the Father, yet the Holy Spirit makes us nervous because we don't know what He will do, when He will do it, and how He will do it.

Many will blame their uncomfortableness with the Holy Spirit on Charismatics and Pentecostals, and on the perceived disorder and chaos of their meetings. Some will reference speaking in tongues as the source of their not wanting to embrace the Holy Spirit. Yet I'm convinced that it's ultimately our lack of control, our inability to define Him, or our inability to put Him in a box that unnerves us. Even the ones who are Charismatic and pray in tongues don't have a clue of whom we are dealing with because praying in tongues is the easy part.

What happens when the Holy Spirit begins to invade our inner world and confronts pockets of rebellion and independence that have never been touched or confronted before?

That's when things get real.

What happens when He confronts small lies, cheating, and deception?

I liken Him to the drunk uncle at Christmas. Most of us have that uncle in the family who drinks a little too much and tends to "ruin" Christmas. Usually, we will quarantine him in some back room, bring his meals to him, and just keep him calm because of one big fear—the fear that he will come out of the back room and begin to expose every dysfunction and relational tension in the family.

God forbid the uncle came out and began to highlight issues between mother-in-law and daughter-in-law, father and son, mother and daughter, or daughter-in-law and daughter-in-law. We would rather have a nice Christmas dinner with our dysfunction than the ugly truth of facing reality in the family.

I can feel the Holy Spirit's zeal, tenacity, and determination in this season to come and rearrange furniture within our lives and our churches to prepare a place for Jesus once again.

The Holy Spirit will first disrupt and confront in order to bring us into a submission and unity.

THE BAPTIZER IN THE HOLY GHOST AND FIRE

I have been hearing the Holy Spirit whisper something else in 2019. He has been saying, "The baptism of fire is here, and it's coming." As John the Baptist said, *"I indeed baptize you with water; but One mightier than I is coming, whose sandal strap I am not worthy to loose. He will baptize you with the Holy Spirit and fire"* (Luke 3:16).

In all four Gospels, this revelation of Jesus is referenced. This may shock you, but this is the most highlighted revelation of Jesus that John carried. More than "Lamb of God" or "Bridegroom," Messiah is One who *"will baptize you with the Holy Spirit and fire."*

John continued by saying that this One will thoroughly clean out His threshing floor. He will store His wheat and will burn the chaff with fire (see Luke 3:17). The baptism of fire comes to remove all of the gray areas and brings separation between the wheat and the chaff. This is a fire of separation, of consecration, and of judgment.

John told the crowds, "My baptism can only prepare you for Him and will clean the outside, but He is going to get up into your business and release fire. His fire will get where the water can't get, and it will remove all hindrances."

It's in the fire where we see Jesus' longing to be closer to us. He is the Bridegroom who longs and desires to get closer, but He must first prepare before He invades.

I believe we've been seeing the preparatory work of this fire over the last several years. It has looked like God has been putting His favorite ones in the fire. The fire has exposed every weakness and vulnerability, and it has brought everything to the surface. This is part of the preparation for us for the outpouring of fire.

Jesus is going to present to Himself a Bride without spot or wrinkle. He gets the spots out through water, but He gets the wrinkles out through fire.

This fire will begin to get to the places that religion could never get to, and I believe it's here where bridal identity and the spirit of prayer are formed.

In Luke 12:49-53, we see one of the core purposes of Jesus' coming to the earth, and it comes out of His own mouth. With six months to go before the cross, we catch another one of those rare glimpses into the soul of Jesus and His longing to be closer to us. He said,

> *I came to send fire on the earth and how I wish it were already kindled! But I have a baptism to be baptized with, and how distressed I am till it is accomplished! Do you suppose I came to bring peace on earth? I tell you, not at all, but rather division. For from now on five in one house will be divided: three against two, and two against three. Father will be divided against son and son against father, mother against daughter and daughter against mother, mother-in-law against her daughter-in-law and daughter-in-law against her mother-in-law.*

Can you feel His longing in this passage? Can you see His longing?

Jesus wasn't avoiding the cross but was eagerly anticipating His own baptism into death so that He could release the fire of the Holy Spirit on His disciples. There was a joy set before Him, and it was the joy of greater intimacy with His people. He longed to be closer to them. He longed to be in them, and He couldn't stand the distance any longer.

Jesus came to send fire, and this fire would not initially bring peace but division. I don't hear anyone talking about the Jesus who came to bring division so we could have true peace with Him and one another. That's the nature of His fire. It first exposes, confronts, divides, and judges so that we can have true compatibility with Jesus and each other.

Jesus lets us know that His fire brings division, and from now on, family members will be set against each other in a way that they hadn't before.

What is Jesus talking about?

He was letting us know that the nature of His fire is that it will get in between the most intimate of relationships for the purpose of God having you for Himself. He won't share you with another but claims full ownership over you.

The unity of the Church with the Holy Spirit will first experience division as God begins to release His fire in increasing measure. This fire will divide but unto the purpose of true unity—not unity built on sentiment and cheap slogans, but reality in humility.

We will only unify with the Spirit to the degree we submit to Him. He will first confront us before He conforms us.

HOW DO WE GROW IN INTIMACY WITH THE HOLY SPIRIT?

There are three ways you can develop greater intimacy with the Holy Spirit:

1. Meditation in the Word (whispering Bible verses to Jesus)
2. Talking to the Holy Spirit
3. Praying in the Holy Spirit

When reading and meditating on the Bible, there will be times that a verse or a phrase jumps off the page, revealing something of God's nature, heart, or ways. When those times happen, simply stop, exhale, and whisper the verse back to God.

Wait in His presence and continue to whisper it. You will notice His presence will increase.

I have found that the Holy Spirit rides on the Word of God. When you intermingle whispering Bible verses to Jesus, talking to the Holy Spirit, and speaking in tongues, He begins to release divine thoughts, divine emotions, Bible verses, burdens, clarity, conviction, and a host of other things.

The last verse of Second Corinthians says, *"The grace of the Lord Jesus Christ, and the love of God, and the communion* [fellowship] *of the Holy Spirit be with you all. Amen"* (13:14).

How do we fellowship or commune with the Holy Spirit?

By talking to Him. By looking at Him. By listening to Him.

The first secret to fellowshipping with the Holy Spirit is by recognizing the fact that He is with you and by slowing down to behold Him with the eyes of faith. It takes time to learn how to slow down and behold Him.

As we come to the place of seeing and sensing Him, we then begin to whisper phrases to Him.

- "Holy Spirit, I love You."
- "Holy Spirit, I bless You."
- "Holy Spirit, I honor You."
- "Holy Spirit, thank You for dwelling within me."
- "Holy Spirit, reign over my thought life, emotions, and desires."
- "Holy Spirit, strengthen me."

Phrases like these with pauses in between begin to create dialogue with Him. Sometimes, He will speak in your thoughts and in your emotions. Sometimes, He will speak Bible verses. In any event, just keep listening and responding to Him. Talk to Him, and expect Him to talk back.

You can pray in tongues as well. Praying in tongues brings you into unity with the Holy Spirit and, thereby, unity with Jesus and the Father.

Praying in tongues:

- Makes a connection with Abba.

- Increases the Spirit of Revelation.

- Strengthens your inner man.

- Magnifies God.

- Stabilizes your emotions and thoughts.

- Builds your faith.

- Increases holiness.

- Increases love for the Bible.

- Increases love for Jesus.

- Increases obedience to Jesus.

- Increases your character and integrity.

- Tames your tongue.

- Opens up a door for other gifts.

I could go on and on and on concerning the benefits of speaking in tongues. I believe the devil has worked overtime to make speaking in tongues the dividing line in Church history because he understands the power it possesses and the destruction it releases on the kingdom of darkness.

I see historic walls crumbling that have divided the Body of Christ. I believe we are about to see an explosion of believers engaging God in tongues.

THE HOLY SPIRIT: YOUR WEDDING PLANNER

The ultimate "Friend of the Bridegroom" is the Holy Spirit. His primary job is telling you what He hears from the Father and the Son. He glorifies Jesus, making known the deep things of Jesus to our spirits. He reveals Jesus to the depths of us, all the while awakening love for the Son of God.

As the Holy Spirit continues to reveal Jesus to us, we will see Jesus and long for Him.

At the beginning of our journey of intimacy with the Holy Spirit, He will deconstruct, tear down, uproot, and destroy wrong paradigms of God and ourselves. More specifically, He begins to remove religious harshness, self-righteousness, independence, arrogance, and pride that all of us possess.

As we persevere in the journey, tenderness, sensitivity, receptiveness, and bridal identity are awakened. Fellowshipping with the Holy Spirit teaches us to slow down, receive, and commune versus rushing in and out of His presence. In time, our tongues shift into a bridal heavenly language of communion, and He begins to shift our relationship with the Father and the Son. It's here that our bridal identity is established. The Holy Spirit changes the way we see God, hear God, and relate to God.

Many people aren't aware of the fact that the Holy Spirit is our wedding gift from the Father. He is the guarantee, the dowry from the Father, ensuring our betrothal to Jesus. He is our assurance that we are His and that there is a day of consummation coming.

Paul tells us in Romans 8:15 that we have received the *"Spirit of adoption by whom we cry out 'Abba, Father.'"* The core work of the Holy Spirit is to establish us in the fact that we belong to God. We are His. This produces security, stability, and identity as sons, daughters, and the Bride.

The Holy Spirit is doing in you today what will set you up for success for billions of years. The areas He's confronting, exposing, and uprooting in you today are for the purpose of your eternal calling as the Bride.

In Revelation 19, we see that the Bride has readied herself. At first glance, this could feel as if what she has done is works-based, but what it actually is highlighting is the fact that she submitted to the process of preparation which the Holy Spirit worked in her life. The Bride didn't give up, back down, or run, but fully submitted to the Holy Spirit as He got out the spots and wrinkles in her life.

How we come into the unity of the Holy Spirit is by submitting to the Holy Spirit. This is going to bring the Church to rest in God and bring His rest to us.

This unity with the Holy Spirit coupled with our bridal identity is going to release a deep anointing of the spirit of prayer.

What is going to happen when the nitric acid of the Holy Spirit meets the glycerol of the Bride?

It will be an explosion called the cry of the Spirit within the Church—*"Come!"*

Right now, this is a whisper, but it's going to culminate into a global roar that will provoke and hasten the Son of God to return.

We will pray.

In light of Revelation 22:17, I believe that our pulpits, Bible study groups, and worship songs will serve to awaken and equip the Church in the Person and the ministry of the Holy Spirit, our bridal identity, and the life and spirit of prayer.

We haven't even begun to hear the messages, read the books, or sing the songs that will come forth to take the Church into these realities.

God will use messengers to prepare and equip the Church for these days, but it will be God who will make it all happen.

10

VOICES NOT ECHOES

FOR THE LAST COUPLE OF YEARS, I'VE KEPT HEARING THE Holy Spirit shout, "The baptism of fire is here, and it's coming!"

Friend, I don't care how gifted you are, how anointed you are, how smart you are, or how skilled you are. The only thing that I desire to know from you is this: Do you want reality?

Are you satisfied with being associated with ministries and gifted people, or do you long to encounter God for yourself?

Are you satisfied with dancing around other people's fires, or do you want to get *into* the fire?

I don't know about you, but I don't want to be an echo. I want to be a voice.

In our noisy, chaotic culture in and out of Church, voices are the desperate need of the hour. We need voices that didn't learn their messages from a man or from a book. We need voices that, in the wilderness of prayer and fasting, heard the Voice from Heaven.

It's going to require great courage to withdraw to the place where all the facades are stripped away and our insecurities and fears are exposed. It's going to take courage to stay in that naked and vulnerable place where we hear God say, "You are Mine."

In an hour where our culture gauges the popularity and authority of a person based on their Instagram follows, Facebook likes, and YouTube views, I can hear the Spirit of God saying, "Come away from all the noise, and buy reality from Me."

Buying reality from God will cost you, but I promise you, when you open your mouth, angels will move, devils will move, and the hearts of men and women will move.

As I stated in chapter 2, God used Isaiah 40 to mark my life and call me into ministry. I believe that this chapter is a must for all messengers.

I have a deep conviction that the Church needs more than polished communicators who know how to "relate." The Church is in desperate need of voices that release words that can actually penetrate the overly saturated culture of perpetual words and images. These kinds of words are born outside time in the place of silent meditation in the Word of God.

The need is great for a new generation of messengers to go through old gates of prayer, fasting, and meditation in the Word to issue words that cut, convict, and expose while healing and delivering people.

We will not get these words at a drive-thru of convenience-driven Christianity, but they will be slowly made flesh in us as we allow the scalpel of the Word of God to divide soul from spirit, as we allow the fire of the Word of God to burn the chaff of sin, as we allow the hammer of the Word of God to break the rock of our hearts, and as we allow the water of the Word of God to wash the defilement out of our lives.

The wilderness is the place where the Word arrests us and subdues us so that it may make its home in us. The ones who have stayed long enough for the Word to become flesh in them will be the voices.

The ones who have allowed the Word to prepare the highway of God inside them will be used to bring words that prepare others for His glory in the earth.

> *The voice said, "Cry out!" And he said, "What shall I cry?" "All flesh is grass, and all its loveliness is like the flower of the field"* (Isaiah 40:6).

If there was one revelation that I believe needs to be restored to this generation of believers, it's the revelation of eternity. Nothing will deliver us from the fleeting opinions, thoughts, and words of this age like the revelation of eternity.

Nothing will deliver us from the fear of man like the revelation of eternity.

Nothing will deliver us from the fading beauty and seduction of our culture like the revelation of eternity.

When believers are immersed in an eternal perspective, we are freed from the inward chaos of proving and defending ourselves.

I'm convinced the only words that are going to be able to penetrate the noisy and wordy generation that we live in will be words born out of eternity.

The wilderness delivers us from the temporal value system and connects us to eternity.

PREACHERS OF THE KNOWLEDGE OF GOD

I believe that God is going to raise up tens of thousands of apostolic and prophetic messengers across the earth to proclaim the majesty of God.

In *The Knowledge of the Holy,* A.W. Tozer spoke of what would happen if one of the holy ones or burning creatures were to come to the earth:

> And were such a one to speak on earth would he not speak of God? Would he not charm and fascinate his hearers with rapturous descriptions of the Godhead? And after hearing him could we ever again consent to listen to anything less than theology, the doctrine of God? Would we not thereafter demand those who would presume to teach us that they speak to us from the mount of divine vision or remain silent altogether?[10]

Friend, I want you to know that there is a holy invitation being given to you right now into the great blue ocean of the knowledge of God. There is a realm of encounter awaiting you, where the Spirit of revelation possesses you and you don't just speak what you've read, but you speak what you've seen and heard in what you've read like John the Baptist: *"There was man sent from God, whose name was John"* (John 1:6).

We are going to see a restoration of preaching that confronts people, but the confrontation is not just highlighting people's stuff, but it is going to go to a higher place of anointed proclamation of God.

Isaiah 40 is God's message to the pride and arrogance of man, and it's primarily about the majesty of God. I believe that, when vessels are so immersed in the revelation knowledge of the majesty of God and then they open their mouths, the spirit of glory and conviction will confront every mountain of arrogance and pride in man. This message will remove all complaining, accusation, and cursing of God in the human heart.

> *Who has measured the waters in the hollow of His hand, measured heaven with a span and calculated the dust of the earth in a measure? Weighed the mountains in scales and the hills in a balance?* (Isaiah 40:12)
>
> *Have you not known? Have you not heard? Has it not been told you from the beginning? Have you not understood from the foundations of the earth? It is He who sits above the circle of the earth* (vv. 21-22).
>
> *He will also blow on them, and they will wither* (v. 24).

The God of Genesis 1 is coming, and Genesis 1 testifies of His glory and His majesty. The God who measures the heavens, weighs the mountains, and measures the waters is the same God who has set His affection upon us, and no one can oppose His will. There is one group of people in the whole earth who has access to His divine resource: people who are in touch with their need or weakness.

The messengers who God is raising up will proclaim the majesty of God in a way that addresses the two greatest and most common lies of the human experience: (1) "God, where are You?" and (2) "God, why aren't You answering my prayer?"

> *Why do you say, O Jacob, and speak, O Israel: "My way is hidden from the Lord, and my just claim passed over by my God"? Have you not known? Have you not heard? The everlasting God, the Lord, the Creator of the ends of the earth, neither faints nor is weary. His understanding is unsearchable* (Isaiah 40:27-28).

God has reserved all of His resource, wisdom, and power for one group: weak, powerless people who exchange their weakness for His power. He actually increases might to those who have none to begin with.

> *He gives power to the weak, and to those who have no might He increases strength. Even the youths shall faint and be weary, and the young men shall utterly fall, but those who wait on the Lord shall renew their strength; they shall mount up with wings like eagles. They shall run and not be weary, they shall not walk and not faint* (Isaiah 40:29-31).

Waiting on the Lord is the occupation of the messenger. We exchange our resource for His. This releases supernatural strength and grace for us to go hard for a long time. This waiting entwines us around God. The priestly waiting unifies your mind, heart, and life with God's. In this place, His divine resources manifest in you and through you, and you are able mount up, run and not wear out, and walk and not faint.

My heart cries out from its depths for you right now— that God would lay hold of your life and take you into His holy heart, forming you into a shepherd who would feed this starving generation with the knowledge of God. It is a lonely journey in many ways, but I promise you will discover that He is with you every step of the way.

> *God, I pray, raise up millions across the earth who know You, who feel You, who manifest You, and who proclaim You. Prepare the highway in the nations for Your coming. Lord, teach us to pray!*

Friend, I bless you and carry you in my heart and my prayers. Let's do this!

ENDNOTES

1. Leonard Ravenhill, *Why Revival Tarries* (Minneapolis: Bethany House, 1987), 25.

2. Leonard Ravenhill, "Wood, Hay, and Stubble," Sermonindex.net video, 0:14, May 23, 2008, http://www .sermonindex.net/modules/myvideo/photo.php?lid=529/.

3. Leonard Ravenhill, *Why Revival Tarries* (Minneapolis: Bethany House, 1987), 20.

4. Deyan G., "33 Out Of This World Video Games Industry Statistics In 2020," techjury, April 23, 2019, https://techjury .net/stats-about/video-games-industry/#gref/.

5. Maryam Mohsin, "10 Social Media Statistics You Need to Know in 2020 [Infographic]," Oberlo, November 7, 2019, https://www.oberlo.com/blog/social-media-marketing -statistics/.

6. Korin Miller, "Adulthood now begins at age 24, say scientists," yahoo! lifestyle, January 19, 2018, https://www .yahoo.com/lifestyle/adulthood-now-begins-age-24-say -scientists-200137174.html/.

7. Wikipedia, s.v. "Holy Club," last modified March 20, 2020, 07:26, https://en.wikipedia.org/wiki/Holy_Club/.

8. Art Katz, *Apostolic Foundations: The Challenge of Living an Authentic Christian Life* (Jupiter, FL: Real Truth Publications, 2017), Introduction, Kindle.

9. Charles H. Spurgeon, 1834-1892, "Inaugural Address at the Sixteenth Annual Conference of the Pastors' College Association, by the President, C. H. Spurgeon," The Sword and the Trowel (London: Passmore & Alabaster), June, 1880.

10. A. W. Tozer, *The Knowledge of the Holy* (New York: HarperCollins, 1961), 71.

ABOUT THE AUTHOR

Corey Russell's passion is to awaken the Church across the earth to the beauty of Jesus, intimacy with the Holy Spirit, and the power of prayer. He has written six books and released five prayer albums. He and his family spent eighteen years in Kansas City, MO with International House of Prayer and is currently on the staff of Global Upper Room based in Dallas, TX. He has been married to his wife Dana for over twenty years and has three daughters and one son.

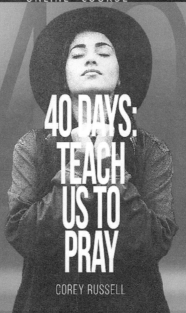

40 DAYS: TEACH US TO PRAY

COREY RUSSELL

HAVE YOU EVER DESIRED TO GROW IN YOUR PRAYER LIFE, BUT NOT KNOWN HOW TO START?

Or perhaps you have a thriving prayer life, but long to connect with others going in the same direction? Maybe you have you hit walls, blocks, and dry spells in your prayer life and wished you had some keys to help get over them? I've had all these same questions, and I've been in the same place, wishing I had keys to help me through some of my driest and most difficult times in prayer. It's with these questions in mind that this course is formed: **40 days of exploring what the disciples requested of Jesus: "Teach us to pray."**

I have spent over 20 years focusing on developing my prayer life and I want to help, encourage, and strengthen as many people as possible to do the same. This online class is to help everyone—whether you have no prayer life, a weak prayer life, or a vibrant prayer life—I believe there is always more! In this class, we will touch on subjects such as seeing God as our Father, and us as His sons and daughters. We will talk on intimacy with the Holy Spirit as He helps us to pray, and how to persevere when we hit walls, blocks, and dry spells in our prayer life. We will look at the prayer of faith, praying in the Spirit, praying the Bible, praying with others, praying alone, and getting a vision to change your world and the world around you through prayer.

I WANT TO INVITE YOU TO JOIN ME ON THIS 40 DAY JOURNEY!

Go to coreyrussellonline.com for all the details

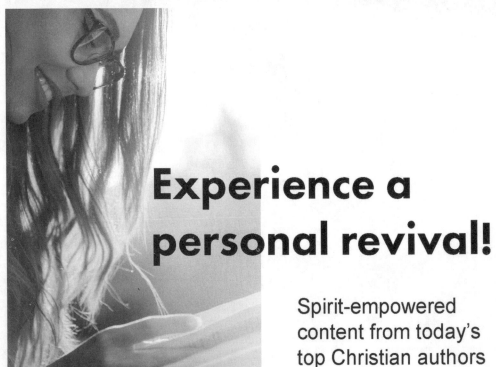